Traveling America
with Today's Poets

Traveling America
with Today's Poets

EDITED BY DAVID KHERDIAN

Macmillan Publishing Co., Inc.
New York

Cop. a

Macmillan Publishing Co., Inc.
866 Third Avenue, New York, N.Y. 10022
Collier Macmillan Canada, Ltd.

Printed in the United States of America

10 9 8 7 6 5 4 3 2 1

LIBRARY OF CONGRESS CATALOGING IN PUBLICATION DATA
Main entry under title:
Traveling America with today's poets.
    Includes index.
    SUMMARY: Presents the moods and aspects of America through the eyes of more than 100 poets.
    1. American poetry—20th century. [1. United States —Poetry. 2. American poetry—20th century—Collections] I. Kherdian, David.
PS613.T7   811'.5'08032   76–47535
ISBN 0–02–750260–0 lib. bdg.

ACKNOWLEDGMENTS

Thanks are due to the following for permission to include copyrighted poems:

Philip Appleman for "Memo to the 21st Century," first published in *Chicago Tribune Magazine*, and collected in his OPEN DOORWAYS, W. W. Norton, copyright © 1976 by Philip Appleman.

James Applewhite, and with the permission of the editor, *Shenandoah: The Washington and Lee University Review,* for "My Grandfather's Funeral," from his STATUES IN THE GRASS, the University of Georgia Press. Copyright 1966 by *Shenandoah,* copyright © 1975 by the University of Georgia Press.

Atheneum Publishers for "Coming Home" by Philip Levine, from his THEY FEED THEY LION, first published in *The Hudson Review* and in 5 DETROITS, Unicorn Press. Copyright © 1968, 1969, 1970, 1971, 1972 by Philip Levine.

William L. Bauhan, Publishers, for Dionis Coffin Riggs' "The Clamdigger," from MARTHA'S VINEYARD, copyright © 1965, 1972; and Allan Block's "Causeway," from his IN NOAH'S WAKE, copyright © 1972 by Allan Block.

Jim Barnes for "A Choctaw Chief Helps Plan a Festival in Memory of Pushmataha's Birthday," first published in *Lake Superior Review*, copyright © 1977 by Jim Barnes.

Bruce Bennett Brown for "The Return," copyright © 1977 by Bruce Bennett Brown.

Harold Bond for "Letters from Birmingham," first published in *The North American Review*, and collected in his book DANCING ON WATER, The Cummington Press, copyright © 1969 by Harold Bond.

David Bottoms for "Writing on Napkins at the Sunshine Club" and "Faith Healer Come to Rabun County," copyright © 1977 by David Bottoms.

Black Sparrow Press for Charles Bukowski's "Another Academy," from his MOCKINGBIRD WISH ME LUCK, copyright © 1972 by Charles Bukowski.

John Brandi for "How to Get to New Mexico," copyright © 1977 by John Brandi.

Lillie D. Chaffin for "Tourism," first published in *Poetry II*, copyright © 1977 by Lillie D. Chaffin.

Leo Connellan for "Watching Jim Shoulders," from his PENOBSCOT POEMS, first published in *The Nation,* and collected in his PENOBSCOT POEMS, published by John Baringer with New Quarto Editions, and FIRST SELECTED POEMS, University of Pittsburgh Press. Copyright © 1974, 1976 by Leo Connellan.

Gerald Costanzo for "The Man Who Invented Las Vegas," first published as a broadside by Rook Press, Derry, Pa., copyright © 1976, 1977 by Gerald Costanzo.

Art Cuelho for "My Own Brand," copyright © 1977 by Art Cuelho.

Crown Publishers, Inc., for Millen Brand's "Longing for the Persimmon Tree," from his LOCAL LIVES, copyright © 1975 by Millen Brand.

R. P. Dickey for "Santo Domingo Corn Dance," first published in *Quetzal*, copyright © 1977 by R. P. Dickey.

D. W. Donzella for "The Last Job I Held in Bridgeport," first published in *Red Fox Review*, copyright © 1977 by D. W. Donzella.

E. P. Dutton & Co., Inc., for Miller Williams' "Alcide Pavageau" and "Plain," from his THE ONLY WORLD THERE IS, copyright © 1968, 1969, 1970, 1971 by Miller Williams.

Dave Etter for "A House by the Tracks," from his GO READ THE RIVER, copyright © 1966 by the University of Nebraska Press, and "The Fighter," from VOYAGES TO THE INLAND SEA, copyright © 1971 by John Judson.

Christopher Fahy for "Miss Ada" and "Bunny." "Miss Ada" was first published in *Maine Times*. Copyright © 1977 by Christopher Fahy.

Clyde Fixmer for "Canal Street, Chicago," first published in *Images* as "Tenement," in a different version. Copyright © 1977 by Clyde Fixmer.

The Four Seasons Foundation for Edward Dorn's "Chronicle" and "When the Fairies," from his COLLECTED POEMS: 1956–1974, copyright © 1975 by Edward Dorn.

John Garmon for "Old Trail Town," copyright © 1977 by John Garmon.

The Giligia Press for David Kherdian's "When These Old Barns Lost Their Inhabitants and Then Their Pain and Then All Semblance of Determined Human Construction," from his LOOKING OVER HILLS, copyright 1972 by David Kherdian; and Steven Lewis's "Fort Wayne, Indiana," from BREWING: 20 MILWAUKEE POETS, copyright 1972 by the Giligia Press.

Dan Gillespie for "Abandoned Copper Refinery," first published in *Chelsea 20/21;* "Desert Gulls," first published in *Kayak;* and "Strip Mining Pit," first published in *Choice;* and all collected in QUICKLY AGING HERE: SOME POETS OF THE 1970'S, edited by Geof Hewitt, copyright © 1969 by Doubleday and Company, Inc. Copyright © 1977 by Dan Gillespie.

Patrick Worth Gray for "Bread Loaf to Omaha, Twenty-Eight Hours," copyright © 1977 by Patrick Worth Gray.

Grove Press, Inc., for Edward Field's "The Statue of Liberty," from his STAND UP FRIEND WITH ME, copyright © 1963 by Edward Field, and for Paul Blackburn's "The Sign," from his THE CITIES, copyright © 1967 by Paul Blackburn.

John Haines for "The Invaders," from his TWENTY POEMS, Unicorn Press, copyright © 1971 by John Haines.

James Baker Hall for "The Mad Farmer Stands Up in Kentucky for What He Thinks Is Right," "The Song of the Mean Mary Jean Machine," "The Modern Chinese History Professor Plays Pool Every Tuesday and Thursday After Dinner with His Favorite Student," and "The Old Athens of the West Is Now a Blue Grass Tour." All but the last, which has not been previously published, are from his book, GETTING IT ON UP TO THE BRAG, Larkspur Press, copyright © 1975 by James Baker Hall.

Sam Hamill for "Reno, 2 a.m.," from his UINTAH BLUE, Copper Canyon Press, and PETROGLYPHS, Three Rivers Press, copyright © 1975, 1976, 1977 by Sam Hamill.

Sam Hamod for "Anthropology in Fort Morgan, Colorado," from his THE FAMOUS BOATING PARTY: POEMS & THINGS, Cedar Creek Press, copyright © 1970 by Sam Hamod.

Harcourt Brace Jovanovich, Inc., for Sheila Cudahy's "Heroes of the Strip," from her THE BRISTLE CONE PINE AND OTHER POEMS, copyright © 1976 by Sheila Cudahy.

Joy Harjo for "The Last Song," from her THE LAST SONG, Puerto Del Sol, copyright © 1975 by Joy Harjo; and "He Told Me His Name Was Sitting Bull," copyright © 1977 by Joy Harjo.

James Hearst for "Behind the Stove" and "The New Calf," from his A SINGLE FOCUS, The Prairie Press, copyright © 1967 by James Hearst.

William Heath for "Cold Feet in Columbus," copyright © 1977 by William Heath.

Holt, Rinehart and Winston for Al Young's "Pachuta, Mississippi/A Memoir," from his THE SONG TURNING BACK INTO ITSELF, copyright © 1965, 1966, 1967, 1968, 1970, 1971 by Al Young.

Quentin R. Howard for "In the Corn Land," copyright © 1977 by Quentin R. Howard.

William Keens for "A Place by the River," first published in UNIVERSITY & COLLEGE POETRY PRIZES 1967–72, edited by Daniel Hoffman, The Academy of American Poets, 1974. Copyright © 1977 by William Keens.

George Keithley for his "Mardi Gras," first published in *The Sweet Thief*, from his book, SONG IN A STRANGE LAND, George Braziller, copyright © 1974 by George Keithley.

Karl Kopp for "The Judge," first published in *amotfa: a magazine of the fine arts*. Copyright © 1977 by Karl Kopp.

Esther M. Leiper for "The Black Bottom Bootlegger," first published in *Heurfano*. Copyright © 1977 by Esther M. Leiper.

Charles Levendosky for "The Gifts" and "The Heart Mountain Japanese Relocation Camp: 30 Years Later." The latter first published in *Poetry in Public Places*, 1976. Copyright © 1977 by Charles Levendosky.

Ray Lindquist for his "On the Land," from his BY-PRODUCTS, A Crossing Press Book, copyright © 1972 by Ray Lindquist.

Liveright Publishing Corporation for Daniel Mark Epstein's "First Precinct Fourth Ward," and "Night Song from Backbone Mountain," from his NO VACANCIES IN HELL, copyright © 1971, 1972, 1973 by Daniel Mark Epstein.

Louisiana State University Press for James Whitehead's "Delta Farmer in a Wet Summer," from his DOMAINS, copyright © 1966 by Louisiana State University Press, and for J. Edgar Simmons' "A Father in Tennessee" (published as "Letter with No Title"), from his DRIVING TO BILOXI, copyright © 1968 by Louisiana State University Press.

Richard Lyons for "The Sisseton Indian Reservation," copyright © 1977 by Richard Lyons.

Macmillan Publishing Co., Inc., for John Beecher's "Desert Holy Man," from his COLLECTED POEMS: 1924–1974, copyright © 1956, 1960, 1962, 1964, 1966, 1974 by John Beecher; and for David Kherdian's "Winter, New Hampshire," from his THE NONNY POEMS, copyright © 1974 by David Kherdian.

Freya Manfred for "For a Young South Dakota Man," copyright © 1977 by Freya Manfred.

David Martinson for "*from* Nineteen Sections from a Twenty Acre Poem," from his BLEEDING THE RADIATOR, *Dacotah Territory*, copyright © 1974 by David Martinson.

Cleopatra Mathis for "Pine Barrens: Letter Home" and "View of Louisiana," copyright © 1977 by Cleopatra Mathis.

Thomas McGrath for "Something Is Dying Here," from his THE MOVIE AT THE END OF THE WORLD: COLLECTED POEMS, The Swallow Press, copyright © 1972 by Thomas McGrath.

The Estate of Stephen L. Mooney for "At the Airport in Dallas," from POETRY SOUTHEAST: 1950–70, edited by Frank Steele, copyright © 1968 by *Tennessee Poetry Journal*, Stephen Mooney, Publisher.

Robert Morgan for "Reuben's Cabin," copyright © 1977 by Robert Morgan.

New Directions Publishing Corporation for Gary Synder's "Marin-An," from his THE BACK COUNTRY, copyright © 1957, 1968 by Gary Snyder, and for his "It Pleases," from his TURTLE ISLAND, copyright © 1974 by Gary Snyder.

New Rivers Press for Victor Contoski's "Moonlit Night in Kansas," from his BROKEN TREATIES, copyright © 1973 by Victor Contoski.

Kell Robertson for "Landscape, New Mexico," "Between a Good Hat & Good Boots," and "Crossing West Texas (1966)," from his THE EYES OF JESSE JAMES, Borracho Press, copyright © 1973 by Kell Robertson; and "Julio," from his ALL THE BAR ROOM POETRY IN THIS WORLD CAN'T MEND THIS HEART OF MINE DEAR, Litmus, copyright © 1974 by Kell Robertson.

Rutgers University Press for John Stone's "An Example of How a Daily Temporary Madness Can Help a Man Get the Job Done," from his THE SMELL OF MATCHES, copyright © 1972 by Rutgers University, the State University of New Jersey.

George Scarbrough for "Tenantry," first published by *The Sam Houston Literary Review*, copyright © 1977 by George Scarbrough.

Richard Schaaf for "Sparkling Water," copyright © 1977 by Richard Schaaf.

James Schevill for "Looking at Wealth in Newport," copyright © 1977 by James Schevill.

Naomi Shihab for "Driving North from Kingsville" and "Jefferson, Texas," the latter first published in *Texas Portfolio*. Copyright © 1977 by Naomi Shihab.

J. Edgar Simmons for "Troubador," copyright © 1977 by J. Edgar Simmons.

Bennie Lee Sinclair for "The Evangelist" and "Decoration Day," from her LITTLE CHICAGO SUITE, copyright © 1971 by The Drummer Press.

Solo Press for Ted Kooser's "Country-Western Music," first published in PRAIRIE SCHOONER, and "Late Lights in Minnesota," from his LOCAL HABITATION & A NAME, copyright © 1974 by Ted Kooser.

John Stone for "Double-Header," first published in *The American Scholar*. Copyright © 1975, 1977 by John Stone.

H. R. Stoneback for "Toad Suck Ferry," copyright © 1977 by H. R. Stoneback.

Floyd C. Stuart for "Settling In," copyright © 1977 by Floyd C. Stuart.

Unicorn Press for Michael Hogan's "Spring," from his LETTERS FOR MY SON, copyright © 1975 by Michael Hogan.

The University of Chicago Press for John Knoepfle's "Riverfront, St. Louis," from his RIVERS INTO ISLANDS, copyright © 1965 by The University of Chicago Press.

The University of Illinois Press for Michael S. Harper's "The Ice-Fishing House: Long Lake, Minnesota," from his HISTORY IS YOUR OWN HEARTBEAT, copyright © 1971 by Michael S. Harper.

The University of Massachusetts Press for Bill Tremblay's "The Court We Live On," from his CRYING IN THE CHEAP SEATS, copyright © 1971 by The University of Massachusetts Press.

University of Missouri Press for Ed Ochester's "The Penn Central Station at Beacon, N.Y.," from his DANCING ON THE EDGES OF KNIVES, copyright 1973 by Ed Ochester; and for R. P. Dickey's "Early June," from his ACTING IMMORTAL, copyright © 1970 by R. P. Dickey.

University of Pittsburgh Press for James Den Boer's "Spring in Washington," from his book LEARNING THE WAY, copyright © 1968 by the University of Pittsburgh Press, and for Jack Anderson's "The Invention of New Jersey," from his book THE INVENTION OF NEW JERSEY, copyright © 1969 by the University of Pittsburgh Press.

University of Washington Press for Jarold Ramsey's "Indian Painting, Probably Paiute, in a Cave Near Madras, Oregon," from his LOVE IN AN EARTHQUAKE, copyright © 1973 by University of Washington Press.

Robert Vander Molen for "In the Bar," to be published in his book ALONG THE RIVER & OTHER POEMS, New Rivers Press, 1977. Copyright © 1977 by Robert Vander Molen.

Mark Vinz for "Primer Lesson," copyright © 1977 by Mark Vinz.

Ramona Weeks for "The Indian Graveyard," first published in POETRY OF THE DESERT SOUTHWEST, edited by James Quick, The Baleen Press, copyright © 1973, 1977 by Ramona Weeks.

Wesleyan University Press for John Haines' "The Train Stops at Healy Fork," from his THE STONE HARP, copyright © 1970 by John Haines; and for David Ray's "Stopping Near Highway 80" and "Dragging the Main," both from his GATHERING FIREWOOD: NEW POEMS AND SELECTED, copyright © 1972, 1974 by David Ray.

John Foster West for "Hill Hunger," copyright © 1977 by John Foster West.

Philip Whalen for "How Was Your Trip to L.A.?" from his ON BEAR'S HEAD, Harcourt, Brace & World, Inc., and Coyote, copyright © 1960, 1965, 1969 by Philip Whalen.

James Whitehead for "The Narrative Hooper and L.D.O. Sestina with a Long Last Line," copyright © 1977 by James Whitehead.

Miller Williams for "Getting Experience," copyright © 1977 by Miller Williams.

Windflower Press for Don Welch's "Funeral at Ansley," first published in *Magazine of the Midlands* (*Omaha World Herald*'s Sunday Supplement), from his DEAD HORSE TABLE, copyright © 1975 by Don Welch, and for Ted Kooser's "Wild Pigs," copyright © 1971 by Ted Kooser.

Barbara Winder for "Cuban Refugees on Key Biscayne," first published in *Chomo-Uri*, copyright © 1977 by Barbara Winder.

Harold Witt for "Rushmore" and "Walking Milwaukee," both first published in *The Hudson Review* and collected in his NOW, SWIM, The Ashland Poetry Press, copyright © 1974 by Harold Witt.

Warren Woessner for "Chippewa Lake Park," "Driving to Sauk City," and "Airwaves." "Driving to Sauk City" first appeared in *Wormwood Review;* "Airwaves" (as "Nocturne") was first published in *The Trojan Horse,* and collected in his THE RIVERS RETURN, copyright © 1969 by Gunrunner Press.

Jackman Young for "Arkansas/I," copyright © 1977 by Teresa Jackman Young.

Preface

To travel *this* America—by page and poem, and not by rail or plane or car or foot—is a special kind of movement, and one that I hope will result in a special kind of insight into this place we call home, by which each of us means: our own corner, cell, neighborhood, community and house. Or family, fraternity, ecology and climate. Since the movement is by page, a word about how I constructed the journey might be in order.

Traveling from East to West (across the North) and returning West to East (across the South) provides a subtle movement in terms of changing climate, mores and speech patterns, with adjustments between place and people the easiest for the reader to make. In this way, the dramatic changes that begin to occur in the West are easier to understand, and help to pave the way for the still greater changes the reader will meet in the Southwest and Deep South.

Whether native or tourist, each of the poets in this book is grounded differently to his or her place. The reader will find here both a cry for change and a lament for the loss of old customs and beliefs. Above all, what these poets are saying—almost unknowingly, it seems—is that although we are one people, we are also a richly diverse nation, sharing in a common humanity but differing radically in speech and stance, attitude and aspiration. How and why this is so is the drama of this book, as the energy that gives this truth its impetus is the book's true subject: America.

David Kherdian

New Concord, New York
August 8, 1976

Contents

WASHINGTON, D.C.

New York City

THE STATUE OF LIBERTY

All the ships are sailing away without me.
Day after day I hear their horns announcing
To the wage earners at their desks
That it is too late to get aboard.

They steam out of the harbor
With the statue of a French woman waving them good-by
Who used to be excellent to welcome people with
But is better lately for departures.

The French gave her to us as a reminder
Of their slogan and our creed
Which hasn't done much good
Because we have turned a perfectly good wilderness
Into a place nice to visit but not to live in.

Forever a prisoner in the harbor
On her star-shaped island of gray stones
She has turned moldy looking and shapeless
And her bronze drapery stands oddly into the wind.

From this prison-like island
I watch the ships sailing away without me
Disappearing one by one, day after day,
Into the unamerican distance,

And in my belly is one sentence: *Set Freedom Free,*
As the years fasten me into place and attitude,
Hand upraised and face into the wind
That no longer brings tears to my eyes.

Edward Field

ANNUNCIATION

Laborers, domestics, blue
collars, unemployed
climb the spit-crusted
stair—up the hairy
legs of lucifer—

to the stink of
pushcart fish, phony
wine from open door
houses that never sleep.

The old man,
wizened black,
hangs over the abyss
between Fulton Street
and the shuttle
to Eastern Parkway.

Into unwilling hands
he pushes the cheap paper
message:
Jesus Saves

If you had made the world,
would you have thought
of that?
a small man
with a broken nose
angel of the annunciation.

Sister Maura, S.S.N.D.

WALKING

I get a cinder in my eye
                    it streams into
      the sunlight
               the air pushes it aside
and I drop my hot dog
                   into one of the Seagram Building's
fountains
          it is all watery and clear and windy

the shape of the toe as
                 it describes the pain
of the ball of the foot,
               walking walking on
asphalt
        the strange embrace of the ankle's
lock
     on the pavement
               squared like mausoleums
but cheerful
          moved over and stamped on
slapped by winds
              the country is no good for us
there's nothing
           to bump into
                or fall apart glassily

there's not enough
            poured concrete
                  and brassy
reflections
        the wind now takes me to
The Narrows
          and I see it rising there
                   New York
greater than the Rocky Mountains

Frank O'Hara

THE SIGN

End of September. At
19th Street and Fifth Avenue
on the sidewalk in front of
the U.S. Employment Service
a colored lady looks at her watch.
Five of nine.
She shines in the sun impatiently

In Madison Square Park
young Persephone from the Bronx
emerges from subway
ducks her head into
the *Daily Mirror,* walks
not hearing the message
in Puerto Rican Spanish
delivered toward her ear
by a passing young man from Third Avenue and 26th St.
Lady!
You're being flirted with—
enter your life!

I wonder,
does this fountain run all night?
The park smells like an autumn hayfield, dried
leaves, dried grass all heaped together to be
burned in hazy afternoons by men
                    with rakes and visor caps.
Sparrow
looks at fountain ambitiously
and settles for puddle next to it, left
from last night's rain.

In another puddle nearby, a big one,
seventeen disreputable-looking pigeons splutter and
splash and duck their heads

and drink and gargle away.
Among them a single warbler
green and tan wings splayed
digs long beak into underbelly
makes his toilet.

It is settled in already
the birds all employed with their hygiene
the unemployed with their newspapers
on street corners or park benches
Persephone with her page 5
young Hermes off on his errand, hopeless
bums preening outside the public facilities,
and center of it all, this
fountain plashes away   And finally
today   there are
more leaves on the surface of the pool than dixie cups
Fall is come

Paul Blackburn

Connecticut

SPARKLING WATER

Like when
I drove one of my students
home . . .
in the ghetto
the North End of Hartford

. . . one room . . . curtains . . .
the bare necessities . . . clean

And when
we walked in
her sister was ironing

"Hi" . . . warm . . . handshakes . . .
"Would you like a glass of water?"

"Yes, thank you"

served up like champagne
the best damn glass of water I ever had

Richard Schaaf

THE LAST JOB I HELD IN BRIDGEPORT

Downtown in the city where I was born
the buses arrive bringing no one,
they leave taking no one away.

At noon I walk through an arcade of abandoned stores,
the hangers waiting like the skeletons of birds,
the windows with dust on their lips.
In that boarded up men's store my uncle bought his last suit.

Five bank buildings
hold up the afternoon sky.

I have half an hour to eat
where winos stalk the leavings
of whoever can still find a job here.

One of them, a woman with a shopping bag
and badly infected legs,
sits so I see them over my sandwich,
the hunger in each of us making her smile.

D. W. Donzella

Rhode Island

LOOKING AT WEALTH IN NEWPORT

Look at wealth through warm, misty rain
And dream American; wander waterfront drives
Staring at mansions of visionary marble,
Renaissance villas oriented east in tribute
Toward the Madonna, Italy; the mistress, France.
Gape with rebellious nostalgia at English
Country estates, fixed, rational order
Where servants serve the idea of service.
Here tennis was invented for the right sports clothes
And Cole Porter composed "Night and Day"
As summer socialites dreamed of community,
Money pursuing happiness in prosperous summers.
Now in these grotesque, vacant mansions
The ghost of Henry James speculates
About the Jolly Corner, where you're haunted
By yourself, the enigmatic observer,
As James's home flickers transformed into a Funeral Parlor.

James Schevill

Massachusetts

THE MODERN CHINESE HISTORY PROFESSOR
PLAYS POOL EVERY TUESDAY AND THURSDAY
AFTER DINNER WITH HIS FAVORITE STUDENT

There they are in the billiard room of the faculty club.
A Chinese boy in a white coat serves them brandy.
The Professor, distinguished in his late forties,

bent over the brilliant felt in the low light,
strokes his cue with passion for the game.
Across the table, in bellbottoms and a floppy hat,
his student holds her cue with both hands like a standard.
She has a full sensual mouth, is writing on Mao in Hunan.
In the shadows against the wall, high kneed on a high chair,
sits the Professor's doughty wife in her overcoat.
She grips her purse and smiles, as though someone were watching,
tries to follow the game, but doesn't know the rules.
The balls click in the basement billiard room of this girls' school,
while upstairs, comfortable and intricate in their learning,
the Professor's colleagues analyze all their sick friends,
discussing at the moment who's the saddest,
the Professor, or his wife, or the young lady.

James Baker Hall

THE COURT WE LIVE ON

The court we live on is a dead end:
a cyclone fence
and then the light and power company

a hundredfoot smokestack
coal burns   the sky is grey sometimes:
all night the transformers hum like locusts
to the sleepless

sitting on the steps I can see them all
the mothers   leaning out over railings
hanging clothes on spiderweb lines
from second-story porches   in housecoats

battling against the soot
screaming across the street "Chris d'Calvie!"
when one kid gets beaten up by another

they wash and cook
and love their husbands one night
throw them out the next, sometimes saying
how they've been to confession to take
communion and no making love
hulking husbands stinking beer

and as if the Church were not enough
they go to a woman's house on Worcester Street
who drops two drops of olive oil   on water
and if they join it is the reason   the evil eye

a lot of them work the second shift
at the American Optical
I see them cutting down the sad path through the coal yard
and theirs is the death of cancerous mothers
and retarded children to be sent away to Belchertown

but mostly   it is   this picture
a mother shaking out a rug
on the back porch on a blue May morning
the month of Mary

she sings some simple song.

                                        Bill Tremblay

WHEN THESE OLD BARNS LOST
THEIR INHABITANTS AND THEN
THEIR PAIN AND THEN ALL SEMBLANCE
OF DETERMINED HUMAN CONSTRUCTION

1.
They began to sway to the
forms of nature, desiring
some final ruin; desiring
some final ruin and return

2.

Their bodies ache and sway
to the rhythms of the
beckoning hills

3.

They carry in their burnt
wood the descending rays
of the setting sun

4.

Their windows are as small
as eyes

5.

They wish again to be a
falling tree

David Kherdian

THE CLAMDIGGER

Louisa, when I offered
To dig up huckleberry bushes
From the swamp
And plant them in your garden
You said no,
You'd risk the sunstroke,
Poison ivy, poison oak,
Just for the sake
Of picking berries in the pasture
Where you could hear the chickadees
Call from the nearby woods,
The scratching of chewinks
In dead brown leaves and sticks;
Or see a striped quail whir up
From her hidden chicks.

By the same token, Louisa,
I would go to Squibnocket for quahaugs,

And wade thigh-deep
In the cold, green water of the creek
That slaps against my boots
And trickles in.
(Don't tell me I'll catch cold!)
I'd feel the clink of hard shells
On my rake, the heft
Of quahaugs in my hand.
I'd smell the wild grapes blooming,
And hear the sea gulls mewing
And the upland plover whistling beyond
The wild-rose edges of the pond.

Dionis Coffin Riggs

New Hampshire

WINTER, NEW HAMPSHIRE

chickadees
round suet balls
winter has come

late day
sun sets
on moose mountain
dark cold
blue sky
deer are moving
on evening's
quiet shoulders

shadowless earth

invisible orion
in the sky

    *

birds in suet
sad wintry song
late day
snow banks the
apple trees
haze down
moose mountain
december fog
drifts
by our window
into sight

    *

snow clouds
slowly lift
off moose mountain

the powdery
snow in their
wake
dust the pines
above the meadow

everything
in all directions
green   white   brown

    *

stillness
snowfall
in the valley
across the mountain
a bird flies
in the cathedral
of the wind

*

white plains
in forest grove
snowshoe tracks
round
pine trees
pass & go

dog barks
off further
hills
echo me home

*

early morning
snow shadows
blue
clouds bank
the sun
on moose mountain
deer tracks
lead away
& into
my life

*

april winter
mud
white &
bone chill
we stop in
tire track ankle
water hollow
to hear first
bear hoots
of spring

David Kherdian

Maine

Christian Scientist, high-buttoned mind,
many never saw your kindness.
You believed no one fell ill without good reason:
sin, dark machinations of the enemy.
But in your eighties you saw a doctor for
your iron ankles swollen underneath
the skirt that nearly touched the floor.
Your heart you kept to yourself,
as always.

You knew every plate and table in the school by name.
Things should last forever if you kept them right.
       "No foolishness," you told the children,
told yourself, "Keep busy."
Your smile at me was thin and white as thread.

Eaten so badly you were no more than a twig,
you signed our petition to end the war—
"If it doesn't mean the enemy will take our churches."

Now you're dead.
Today you come back to Maine, your only lover,
and the bed you left so many years ago.

Last night we had our first snow of the season.

Christopher Fahy

BUNNY

You tied Dick Randall to a tree
and tried to pull his legs off with your truck.
"Stick him on an island by himself
and he'd be okay," Henry said.
"It's people does it to him
—and drink, of course."

When you lived where I live now
you smashed the door in with your fist
to reach the bolt your wife had thrown in fear.
Once inside,
"The dishes come out,
the dog come out
and we all come out."
You laughed through rotted teeth
and threw your empty beer can
on the lawn that used to be your lawn.

A kid could have fixed that door
better than you did,
I had to get a new one.
"That fool calls himself a carpenter,"
your mother said.

But when your blood is cool
the wood sings in your hands,
your hard blue eyes
are deeper than the bay in mysteries.

"Keep everything," you said.
"These boards belong here,
don't let no one take 'em,
burn 'em first.
Don't tear the old barn down
until I die."

You looked at me and said,
"You think I'm crazy."

I remembered
that small bright awkward painting you did
of a lobster boat.
I saw it where your mother hung it
hopelessly
above her kitchen stove.

Christopher Fahy

Vermont

SETTLING IN

Wind licks stray hairs on shiny heads
as the old men, with nail and lathe

and rolls of black paper, wrap foundations up.
Some snug bales of hay against the granite,

the slate. "She'll be an open winter,"
they call to each other, and stretch their rubbery

lips and show their gums at their own joke.
They hammer and hammer, and remember,

almost, what it was to tuck the child in.
Young husbands lurch the heavy storms

up ladders. Their wives ignore the curses.
Even the houses of broken-hipped widows

one day stare down October through double glass.
Whole north walls, sieves of rotted clapboard,

blur under plastic sheets. Wind shimmies
the plastic across front doors, testing

where in a month, two, a finger might
fit in. Finally we say, "Winter can come."

It is not a taunt.

Floyd C. Stuart

New York

THE PENN CENTRAL STATION AT BEACON, N.Y.

An immense room as quiet
as an elephant graveyard
without spines or tusks.
Dust in the slantlight from windows
twenty feet up the wall.
Yesterday's *Times* for sale.
The stationmaster in a green eyeshade
snoozing or dead.
Below the clock an American flag.
Twice a day empty trains
go by without stopping—
Eisenhower Eisenhower Eisenhower Eisenhower—
one-eyed trains twice a night—
FDR & FDR & FDR & FDR—
shuttle between
Albany Albany Albany Albany
Manhattan Manhattan Manhattan Manhattan

Ed Ochester

ON THE LAND

John Deere, Allis Chalmers, Farm-All, Oliver,
    International
Tractors in all directions on the land plowing,
    discing, planting,
Rock and country music over the noise to the drivers
On a June morning
Joyful the more because denied for six tight weeks
    by rain
Waiting to get out on the land, working on unpleasant
    jobs,
Everything waiting, figuring again and again how far
    behind, how far behind,
Now out on the land
Men driving, women driving,
John Deere, Farm-All, Oliver, Massey-Ferguson.

Ray Lindquist

New Jersey

THE INVENTION OF NEW JERSEY

Place a custard stand in a garden
or in place of a custard stand
    place a tumbled-down custard stand
in place of a tumbled-down custard stand
    place miniature golf in a garden
    and an advertisement for miniature golf
        shaped for no apparent reason
        like an old Dutch windmill
in place of a swamp
    place a swamp

or a pizzeria called the Tower of Pizza
   sporting a scale model
      of the Tower of Pisa
or a water tower resembling
   a roll-on deodorant
or a Dixie Cup factory
   with a giant metal Dixie Cup on the roof

In place of wolverines, rabbits, or melons
   place a vulcanizing plant
in place of a deer
   place an iron deer
   at a lawn furniture store
   selling iron deer
      Negro jockeys
      Bavarian gnomes
      and imitation grottoes
      with electric Infants of Prague
in place of phosphorescence
   of marshy ground at night
     place smears of rubbish fires
in place of brown water with minnows
   place brown water

     gigantic landlords
     in the doorways of apartment houses
     which look like auto showrooms
     auto showrooms which look like diners
     diners which look like motels
     motels which look like plastic chair covers
     plastic chair covers which look like
     plastic table covers which look like plastic bags
     the mad scientist of Secaucus
     invents a plastic cover
     to cover the lawn
     with millions of perforations
     for the grass to poke through

In place of the straight lines of grasses
    place the straight lines of gantries
in place of lights in the window
    place lighted refineries
in place of a river
    place the road like a slim pair of pants
        set to dry beside a neon frankfurter
in place of New Jersey
    place a plastic New Jersey

        on weekends a guy has nothing to do
        except drive around in a convertible
        counting the shoe stores
        and thinking of screwing
            his date beside him
            a faintly bilious look
            perpetually on her face

                                    Jack Anderson

Pennsylvania

ED SHRECKONGOST

The two of us roof my house,
canvas aprons weighted down
with tinned nails as we walk inchwise
on our knees across the grit of shingles.
Deciduous mountains, old men
sleeping, lie down all the way to Saltsburg,
here & there the unhealed scars of stripmines.
He keeps a pint in his pocket with the nails,
and late morning we sit astraddle
the ridge pole and pass whiskey back & forth:

"trouble with me is I ain't got an education
like yuns, but I like my time free too—
you ain't work much, but you get by.
Same's me. Cept I'm what you call dog-poor,
got eighteen last count, costs more to feed
than kids. Some's belly always needs fill but—
She-it! last time the tax assessor come
ask me what I'm doin now, told'm
'Verne,
I'm a coonhunter
presently
unemployed.' "
and laughs so hard his hammer
slips from his knee, slides the slant roof
and arcs out gracefully through air.

Ed Ochester

LONGING FOR THE PERSIMMON TREE

She comes up the walk toward her back door, Mama Longacre,
    trailing her shyness over the lawn, so well kept,
    so wonderfully green in the cold morning.
She passes the persimmon-tree stump.
There it sits, a dark wedge like a lump of firewood, with
    the memory of its red fruit in the damp of its slanting
    black rings.
Persimmon Pudding—the recipe's in her kitchen drawer:
    "1 cup persimmon pulp, 1 egg,
    2 tablespoons butter, 1 cup sugar,
    1/2 cup cream (or milk), 1 cup sour milk,
    1 teaspoon baking powder,
    1/3 teaspoon soda, 1 cup flour,
    1 teaspoon cinnamon
        Mix as for cake and bake in a greased and floured
    pan 45 minutes.
                    From Mrs. Henry Hustand."

Such good pudding, Milton liked it so much, and just about
   now, with the first good hard freeze, the persimmons
   turned so soft, sweet, and juicy.
Funny, something that, before the frost, made your mouth
   pucker like alum.
A funny-leaved tree—with bees buzzing in the leaves,
   and the blossoms dropping to the ground like popcorn.
Then a redbird sitting in it like another fruit.
Yes, the tree was forever messing up the ground with twigs and
   branches, and in the fall there was the stain of its
   fruit on the walk—much raking like currying a horse.
But it had become a friend. It seemed to notice her, it seemed
   to shelter her, it seemed to shade her particularly the
   days Milton was away, to New Holland and such.
And its leaves were so funny, so pretty.
The wind had such a sound in it,
such a shining,
not to have it
            now
                any longer.
Ai, ai, Milton must clean the stump down to the ground and I
   must forget it once and for all.
You get old
and friends die.

Millen Brand

Ohio

LABOR DAY

Every Labor Day the two old guys trot out their flags
And hoist them up the poles toward the blue sky
And the sun shines down brightly upon the drunks in
   the park

And the Faulkner family has gone to Kentucky for the
   holiday
And the fat lady her hair in pink curlers sits on her
   porch bellowing Baptist spirituals
And the whites of the houses are white and clean
   as eggshells
And the Kroger store is dark and deserted
And Tom, the neighborhood maniac, hops the bus to
   the Ohio State Fair.

Gary Pacernick

CHIPPEWA LAKE PARK

The bored lifeguard shrugs
as we step over the bent down fence
onto the empty beach, run through the moldy bathhouse
and down the midway.
There's almost no one here.
It's the 4th of July.
The Park's a museum now, filled with decaying exhibits
on the history of Play; rows of toys
we forgot how to use.

Now nothing works in the Funhouse.
It's almost scarier to walk through the dark—
only a faint buzz where King Kong once jumped
out from his cage.
The wavy mirrors are dim and greasy.
In the arcade, Joyce stamps my name
on an aluminum good luck medal
while I waste a dime on a pinball time forgot.

Suddenly a busload of young ghetto kids
falls on the Park like a thunder shower.
They start up bumper cars, grin like the ponies
on the merry-go-round, ride the roller coaster

over and over.
The tired machines pick up speed,
begin to run on life again.
We stop pretending to have fun,
tip out our watery sno-cones
and walk home across the empty
giant parking lot.

Warren Woessner

COLD FEET IN COLUMBUS

I got cold feet in Columbus
in a rented room down where
you can hear the coupling
of freight cars   and the blind man
beats his dog   where the winos
piss out windows or talk
to Jesus in the alley   where
hard men caress cans while
their wives preen in vain   where
they beat a man so bad
he didn't mind being pissed on   where
men disappear near the river
and after one day in the water
the baling wire clings
to bare bone   where the murderer
sleeps with his victim's eyes
under his pillow   down there
I couldn't sleep thinking
of the secret, uncounted corpses
of America   in despair I
wondered where my own body
would be found

I got cold feet in Columbus
in a rented room down where

a man can specialize in loneliness
and I knew I'd been lonely
all my life   that Columbus
is just one more hard town
to make friends in   that
having a room where
there's never anyone but you
is normal   and that there's nothing to do
but sit silent on the unmade bed
look out the dusty window
and make love to death

William Heath

Michigan

COMING HOME, *Detroit, 1968*

A winter Tuesday, the city pouring fire,
Ford Rouge sulfurs the sun, Cadillac, Lincoln,
Chevy gray. The fat stacks
of breweries hold their tongues. Rags,
papers, hands, the stems of birches
dirtied with words.
                    Near the freeway
you stop and wonder what came off,
recall the snowstorm where you lost it all,
the wolverine, the northern bear, the wolf
caught out, ice and steel raining
from the foundries in a shower
of human breath. On sleds in the false sun
the new material rests. One brown child
stares and stares into your frozen eyes
until the lights change and you go
forward to work. The charred faces, the eyes

boarded up, the rubble of innards, the cry
of wet smoke hanging in your throat,
the twisted river stopped at the color of iron.
We burn this city every day.

Philip Levine

IN THE BAR

The man next to me   with grey hair
In his ears
Was being refused another whisky

His shoulder lowered away from mine
He said   you look like you
Could use some money

I said no   he said he
Needed an assistant

He was sick   and soon
Would be entering the hospital
For surgery

He showed me a pistol
In holster
Under his rumpled jacket

Listen
I've got a girl waiting for me at home
She's in bed
I've got whisky and dope

He was pretty craggy

I hate sissies
How about you?

I looked into my glass

He said   I've got to kill a man
Otherwise the big boys
From Chicago . . .

He slit his neck
With his finger

Do you understand?   you
Horses ass

Robert Vander Molen

BREAD LOAF TO OMAHA, TWENTY-EIGHT HOURS

Doing 70 on Interstate 94
In the hot August dusk
My little blue Opel straining
Toward the stink of Hammond visible
On the horizon, I was whistling "Hernando's
Hideaway" (you can sing "Stopping
By Woods on a Snowy Evening"
To it) and thinking what a really
Neat poet (and good-looking)
I am when a tractor-trailer
Loaded with new Cadillacs
Its tattooed driver chewing
A Dutch Master right
Beside me pulled left
I jerked left
Another truck, the gap
Narrowed, smoke poured
From my new Sears Radials
Then I was on the shoulder
And the two truckers were shouting

Speed-trap bulletins across
Lanes, blasting into
The Sunset, and I kneeled, losing
Anchovy pizza, Michelob,
Illusions, I was just another
Old man lost in Michigan,
Trying to reach my wife
And daughter, to write another
Lousy poem, just
Another old man, lost
In America, trying to get home.

Patrick Worth Gray

Indiana

FORT WAYNE, INDIANA 1964

it was late afternoon, october
he looked around, said yeah
we threw the laundry bags
in the open van that seemed
as big and dirty as a coal car
jumped in the cab
and left des plaines, illinois

2 axles
5 speeds on each
when he changed axles
his right hand about to jam
the gears past fifth
left hand jerked
through the wheel
tight on the shaking steel lever
double clutched

pushed the lever down
and with a huge grinding
muscled meshed into sixth
moved into the middle lane
and we were really
off

he told us as we
roared past the first weigh station
that he was 300 pounds overweight
that he was two days late
on the run to west virginia
that he got pissed up in minneapolis
and spent four drunken days
with a city woman
that he didn't have a license
that it was illegal
to pick up hitchhikers
and that insurance men
rode up and down the toll roads
looking for truckers who did.

he was everything
i wanted him to be and me
only 18 years old
from roslyn heights, new york
sitting in a filthy old
rumbling mack truck
with a criminal mind
at the wheel

i almost pissed in my pants
he had no teeth
on the right side
of his mouth where
a fat smelly cigar
fit neatly on his gums,

we rounded chicago
east to gary where we got
our first look at the steel mills
and the shallow sky the color
of bloody phlegm
and then southeast on a two lane
rolling over dark farmland
rolling rumbling and after a while
even the potholes became
part of the monotonous rhythm
the engine straining the wheels
the rumbling on and on
eyes fixed on the bulldog
ripping through the indiana night
he downshifted
pumped the brakes squealing
and then around the turn
we saw a small truck stop
he jumped out dropped the cigar
pulled a big wad from a greasy pocket
"it's the boss's" paid for our food
called a woman in kentucky
told her he'd be there by
morning pushed a small white pill
through his gums
and then seemed to stoke it down
with a new cigar
we were off
again
pounding across indiana
more empty than my room
at home pounding
watching the bulldog
leap and sputter leap
and sputter my head
against the cold window
rattled to sleep banged awake

eyes wide open, hands
grabbing for the dash
the whole truck rocking clanging
speeding on the shoulder
and him laughing,
coughing on the goddam cigar, eased
the truck back on the road
said "just wanted to
make sure yer alive"

i didn't go back to sleep
and later we pulled
into another truck stop
outside fort wayne, indiana
1 o'clock in the morning, he
walked into the shop
bought a complete set
of dark green clothes
threw the old ones out
and told us if we wanted
to get to buffalo we
better get out here.

Steven Lewis

STATE FAIR PIGS

Studded with flies,
they stretch pink
and fat, four to a pen,
snoozing oblivious
of my adoration.
They are so immaculate
I want to stand over them
and shoo the flies
off their perfect bodies,
so plump
I want to nuzzle their teats

and squeeze them awake
to tell them how I feel.

A thousand pounds
of contented pork,
they look spun
from cotton candy,
blending one into the other,
snouts and rumps
fused deep in dreams
of ribbons, perhaps,
or of being hosed down
for the third time today.

They smile
as if being clean
is where it's really at,
and they are so far
into being clean
that nothing can touch them,
not even the knife-hot sun
that hangs overhead
like a spotlight on the fair.

Roger Pfingston

MEMO TO THE 21ST CENTURY

It was like this once: sprinklers mixed
our marigolds with someone else's phlox,
and the sidewalks under maple trees
were lacy with August shade,
and whistles called at eight and fathers walked
to work, and when they blew again,
men in tired blue shirts followed
their shadows home to grass.
That is how it was in Indiana.

Towns fingered out to country once,
where brown-eyed daisies waved a fringe on orchards
and cattle munched at clover, and
fishermen sat in rowboats and were silent,
and on gravel roads, boys and girls
stopped their cars and felt the moon and touched,
and the quiet moments ringed and focused
lakes   moon   flowers.
That is how it was
in Indiana.

But we are moving out, now,
scraping the world smooth where apples blossomed,
paving it over for cars. In the spring,
before the clover goes purple,
we mean to scrape the hayfield, and
next year the hickory woods:
we are pushing on, our giant diesels snarling,
and I think of you, the billions of you, wrapped
in your twenty-first century concrete,
and I want to call to you, to let you know
that if you dig down,
down past wires and pipes
and sewers and subways, you will find
a crumbly stuff called earth. Listen:
in Indiana once, things grew in it.

                                        Philip Appleman

Illinois

A HOUSE BY THE TRACKS

Snow falls, stops, starts again.

Santa Fe Wabash Seaboard

The freight train earth cracks in two.

Nickel Plate Nickel Plate

There are curses on the courthouse wind.

B&O L&N

South of town a farmer has been shot
by a hunter with a Jim Beam face.

Illinois Central Illinois Central
(piggyback piggyback)
Great Northern Great Northern
Pennsylvania Rock Island

Cops are burning up the county roads.

Missouri Pacific

The black branches of mulberry trees
are writing my name on the backs of barns.

Union Pacific Norfolk and Western
Burlington Soo Line Burlington

I have hot coffee on the stove
and fresh doughnuts from the A&P.

Milwaukee Road Nickel Plate
North Western Boston and Maine

I have never been so all alone, so

Erie-Lackawanna

Dave Etter

THE FIGHTER

Nubs Lilly liked to use his fists.
A while back, during a heated discussion
at our fortnightly poker session,
he, as usual, got in the first punch.
But it was also his last one,
because this gas-pump jockey named Sal,
from over in De Kalk County,
quickly laid him out with a left hook.
Later, Nubs had to admit
that he had enough of the fight game
and was not really another up-and-coming
"Two Ton Tony" Galento.

Now it's worse, for he's lifting weights
and talking all the time about Frank Gotch,
Hackenschmidt, and Stanislaus Zbyszco.
He fancies himself a wrestler, you see,
and all his cronies have grown very tired
of being asked to "go a fall or two."
Phil Graham says that if Nubs
keeps on flapping his big yap,
he's going to toss his ass into Illinois Street.
When I tell Nubs this latest bit of news,
he gives me a slow smile and says,
"Strangler" Lilly doesn't like that kind of talk.

Dave Etter

CANAL STREET, CHICAGO

The half-moon slides by clumsily, as if on tracks—
as if it were only a prop,
put up by rich merchants.

Pawnbrokers watch the streets with hundreds of eyes.
Tenement landlords sue for back rents
with voices like the fineprint of loan-contracts.

Here the graves crawl out of their cemeteries
to prowl at night,
looking for clients among the brownstones.

A bum sleeps on a park bench,
another bum steals his shoes,
but tries them on first, as though he were in a store.

Tomorrow drifts into town like a bankrupt
to lose itself in all the anonymous yesterdays,
and in the shadows of women lounging in hallways.

The sun is still here,
low in the sky,
but will not outshine the neon above taverns.

Along the El-tracks, beside brick factories,
the half-moon frowns on the city,
on the faces of tenement children, thin as relief checks.

Clyde Fixmer

Iowa

STOPPING NEAR HIGHWAY 80

We are not going to steal the water tower
in Malcom, Iowa,
just stop for a picnic right under it.
Nor need they have removed the lightbulb

in the city park
nor locked the toilet doors.
We are at peace, just eating and drinking
our *poco vino* in Malcom, Iowa,
which evidently once had a band
to go with its bandstand.
We walk down the street, wondering how
it must be to live behind the shades
in Malcom, Iowa, to peer out,
to remember the town as it was before
the Expressway discovered
it, subtracted what would flow
on its river eastwards and westwards.
We are at peace, but when we go into the bar
in Malcom, Iowa, we find that the aunts
and uncles drinking beer have become
monsters and want to hurt us and we do
not know how they could have ever
taken out the giant breasts
of childhood or cooked the fine biscuits
or have told us anything at all
we'd want to know
for living lives as gentle as we can.

David Ray

BEHIND THE STOVE

It takes more than wind and sleet to
snuff my candle, my god, at my age, a
kitchen intrigue, to be installed among
the pots and pans, not the parlor where
the owner sits, and she's no nymph.
A broken basket of odds and ends,
a dark square owl thick in the shoulders,
blowzy hair, sprung thighs, pads on
flat feet between her cupboards, hoots

from her chair, blows coffee in a saucer,
hoards affection, tires from intercourse
with words. Sure, I know all this, I'm
not blind, but, hell, she charms me and
I decorate her wall, chair tipped back,
a kettle still of use, but not worth
polish, I pat her rump as she goes
past and get a dull poke from an elbow
or knife handle as she scrapes the carrots.
I'm an adulterous bastard, while her
husband cuts wood for my fire I
scratch her itch as hooked by love
as any rooster who has caught his hen,
glad to find a spark among the ashes
and make the time seem warm.

James Hearst

THE NEW CALF

In the basement by the furnace lies
a newborn calf I found, chilled and wet,
in the barn this morning, its mother
a wild-eyed young heifer frantic in
the pain of her first birth didn't
lick it off to dry its hair and kicked
it in the gutter when it tried to suck.
I picked it up, rubbed it down and
fed it from a bottle. Here it lies
in a basket lined with straw while
I watch its heart tremble, flanks quiver,
muzzle twitch, eyes flicker. I had to spoon
the milk (mixed with a little brandy)
in its mouth and stroke its throat
to make it swallow, it sucked so feebly
on my finger. Now it waits for life
to decide whether to go or stay—and

I think of deserted innocence everywhere,
a child locked out of the house,
a woman dirtied in love,
a father betrayed by his son, all of us
sometime abandoned, lonely, denied.

James Hearst

Wisconsin

DRIVING TO SAUK CITY

This land won't lie down
like a nice dog after a beating.
It keeps coming back.

Hot. Cold. Empty.

Men wear out,
take their families into town for good.

The skeleton of a Lutheran church
gathers a congregation of young maples.
The graveyard has stopped growing
and gone to seed.

Brick walls last a long time
even by themselves.

The windmill still turns
but someone pulled up the pipe
and shot the cistern full of holes.

Warren Woessner

WALKING MILWAUKEE

At the end of everything, I walk Milwaukee
between the elms cathedraling the blocks
and hotbox houses in the muggy weather—
over to Sherman, or drive to Brown Deer Park.
No one is there to glide the moss but ducks
and under birch and willow only us

to walk in clover, sweating as we walk
with Grandma and the babies by the pond—
who would have thought, in summer hot Milwaukee,
we'd find green vacancies at six o'clock?—
but yesterday I saw a rabbit hop,
as if through grass, across a concrete street

as I was walking, thinking as I walked,
and saw a squirrel flitting up a trunk
while fattened housewives talked among their lawns—
this One Way flatness wildly overflowing
its sober German rules and regulations—
madness of beer, preponderance of paunch.

I walk the miles of square and ugly blocks
scanning the bricks for out of place clematis—
a purple tropic climbing up a string—
drive miles to look at Wright's Greek Orthodox
crown round church, beneath whose darkblue dome,
above eye windows, thorns are watersprouts—

a far out marvel; no one would have thought
concrete could flow so rightly in a ring
except a mind in bitter anguish caught
seeing such blocks of boxed-in suffering—
SCHLITZ signs sizzle, DON'T WALK goes on and off
at this hot endless end of everything.

Past Silver Spring—the names sound meadow cool—
we walk and talk on Grandpa's clovered grave—
death of a salesman—Grandpa sold the lots—
the carving on the stone is "beautiful"—
we talk above him on Valhalla's plots,
smelling the smoke from backyard barbecues—

who will lie where when similarly boxed;
a later generation climbs the stones
over the rigid burghers locked below.
Grandma says the trees, because the roots
would crack the coffins, can't be planted close.
Whom are the plastic flowers meant to fool?

I have to walk—through smogs of Fond du Lac—
the name is lovely but the street goes on
past smoke black bricks, past churches pointing up
to nothing but a boiling murkiness—
thundering dark about to split and drop
gutterflooding water that won't help—

the lightning seems to dramatize a god
whose wise displeasure makes the hailstones bounce,
but soon it's over and I walk again
through heated green beside Menominee River—
(along the banks, because of antique drains
polluting purity, dead fish glitter)—

and on and on, beside the dying elms
(a blight is killing them the city over)
arching a Paradise, to hear Grandma tell,
under the willows, in the parks of clover
I walk Milwaukee in the still hot weather
and think of Dante sweating through his hell.

Harold Witt

Minnesota

1)
How the kerosene outlasted
those weeks of watered solitude
the wind whirled its way
even to the lamp chimney
alone with a borrowed knife
I shaped a whistle from a horse's tooth
and blew from kitchen to chicken coop

wiew   wiew

if you don't like the water you can walk to the well

4)
Where pollen crusts the pine bough
a crow nests in moonlight
crow eyes skirt the grainfield
'ťťťťťťťt

the all-gathering coon
in the all-fathering corn

8)
It's come to this
blue shadows piling in the corner
bird nests as small as cufflinks on the spice rack
little mariahs rising from the stove

it's come so fast
how can I tell you the difference
snow peas lengthen in the garden

a rabbit skirts with no desire
little dandelion puffs drift against the window screen

12)
All morning I watched
the mourning dove lade stick on stick
I've built a furnace of credit cards
it's hard arguing with the vice-president
of the First National Bank
but I did this
I built a fire and dowsed a fire
with these words :

> let olives sprout
> from nests of widowed birds

19)
Sharpening grandpa's scythe
I set out on the north forty
beginning at the end of the road
I mow a new one where I walk

sickled foxtail sweeping through the grass
come one, come all, the oven's full of bread

David Martinson

LATE LIGHTS IN MINNESOTA

At the end of a freight train rolling away,
a hand swinging a lantern.
The only lights left behind in the town
are a bulb burning cold in the jail,
and high in one house,
a five-battery flashlight
pulling an old woman downstairs to the toilet
among the red eyes of her cats.

Ted Kooser

THE ICE-FISHING HOUSE:
LONG LAKE, MINNESOTA

Checking the traps
on the way out
along the iced beaches
the birches sift,
connecting a groundwork
overcome without woman,
this particular snow.

At the first point
the bunny boots soak
up the foot of water
under snow—
we slip in the single
tracks on thick ice
zigzagging northeast
to the house marked "Schultz."

The three trap doors
prism as we auger down,
sinker, minnow, 28 feet;
the kerosene stove heats
the first crappy bed
and we eat.

This greenhouse is set
on stilts, drawn by snowmobiles
over Thanksgiving;
6x8x6
compass, sextant, wheel
blue light.

Thirty-five crappies in a pail
go with us as we leave this hut;

jackrabbit tracks
cross to the point.
Bunny boot snowshoes or full
fishpail, these traps remain unfilled.

The hollow sounds in this wind,
Kandiyohi, Indian place-names
I've heard in my grandmother's voice
calling the Chippewa in
calling the Chippewa in

Michael S. Harper

North Dakota

SOMETHING IS DYING HERE

In a hundred places in North Dakota
Tame locomotives are sleeping
Inside the barricades of bourgeois flowers:
Zinnias, petunias, johnny-jump-ups—
Their once wild fur warming the public squares.

Something is dying here.
                And perhaps I, too—
My brain already full of the cloudy lignite of eternity . . .

I invoke an image of my strength.
                    Nothing will come.
Oh—a homing lion perhaps
                    made entirely of tame bees;
Or the chalice of an old storage battery, loaded
With the rancid electricity of the nineteen thirties
Cloud harps iconographic blood
Rusting in the burnt church of my flesh . . .

But nothing goes forward:
The locomotive never strays out of the flower corral
The mustang is inventing barbwire the bulls
Have put rings in their noses . . .

The dead here
Will leave behind a ring of autobodies,
Weather-eaten bones of cars where the stand-off failed—

Strangers: go tell among the Companions:
These dead weren't put down by Cheyennes or Red Chinese:
The poison of their own sweet country has brought them here.

Thomas McGrath

THE SISSETON INDIAN RESERVATION

The Sisseton Indian Reservation
is the smallest one in North Dakota.
It is now reserved for birds,
which do not stay long.
Birds make short reservations
at Lake Tewaukon
during the tourist season
when the lake is busy with birds
and with bird watchers,
who look at each other awhile
and then move on,
leaving the water empty
and the government agent,
who is from Nebraska,
to file reports at the headquarters.
He lives on the Reservation,
but he is not an Indian.
No Indians live on the Indian Reservation.
One family lives in the files

of the Reservation in Washington,
but that family one year went North
with the birds as far as Cayuga
and did not return with the birds.

Richard Lyons

South Dakota

PRIMER LESSON

> *"Dakota is everywhere"*—*Tom McGrath*

We are driving through South Dakota
   looking for Buffalo
   looking for wildflowers and monuments.

On the car radio
the President announces that the war is over, it is
really over this time, a peace with honor this time . . .

Everything in South Dakota is moving—
   station wagonloads of tourists in search
      of stone faces
         pickups, semis, tandems
                     old men in tennis shoes
                     on motorcycles
            a bicycle troop of girl scouts.
      Even the dust clouds have wheels.

On the car radio
the President announces that poverty
   has been devalued, that
the military budget has been cut back
   to 150 billion dollars . . .

We are driving through a small town in South Dakota,
the thirtieth small town we have driven through today.
All the small towns in South Dakota look alike.
All the roads in South Dakota look alike.
This is the same small town we have been driving
            through all day!

It has 62 gas stations. 13 MacDonalds stands,
    2 liquor stores—
we have stopped in all 77 locations at once. The name
of this small town is Custer. Every small town
    in South Dakota
is called Custer, or Luther. Some are called
    Wounded Knee.

On the car radio
the President announces that the economic crisis
has been a complete success . . .

We cannot stop driving through South Dakota,
We cannot turn off the car radio
    bristling with salvation music
    and the presidential sacrament.
We cannot find the buffalo, or the wildflowers
only the Gateway to the West Drive-in Theatre
    filled with conestogas
                    and hostiles
            dropping eternally from their ponies
            like cardboard ducks
and John Wayne, 30 feet tall, who signs the treaty—

            speaking impossible sign language
            above the car radio,
            he waves to us
            as we drive past

into the roads that unroll suddenly before us,
into the long Dakota night.

Mark Vinz

RUSHMORE

Rushing to Rushmore, speeding as we read
sphinx comparisons (in the free brochure)
to monumental features of the dead,
we doubted art in such a spacious sculpture

especially done by dynamite and drill,
smirked that workmen with electric hammers
had hacked a factual grandeur from that hill.
We sneered like critics. What did those amateurs,

exploding crude colossi out of stone
know of Cellini and his detailed golds,
David expressive to the very tendon
or marble Grecians rippling in their robes?

And we were anxious on a trip to elsewhere,
winding narrowness, just to glimpse and go.
Then through a tunnel we saw history centered,
staring four faced, bluish in the glow.

Dazzled travelers, skeptic to the end,
we drove up closer, looked in Lincoln's eye
in which a six foot man could easily stand
and, vita brevis, made a longer stay.

We gazed along the precipice of faces,
silenced by a pyramidal shock—
temples, obelisks, the statued ages
were equaled in that democratic rock.

Harold Witt

FOR A YOUNG SOUTH DAKOTA MAN

I no longer want to meet
people who have no muscles.

I love your muscles.
I love the barbwire cuts in your
      tan-gold shoulder,
the rattlesnake skin tied around
      your head,
the way your hands curl like warm rabbits
      beside the campfire.

I planted a lilybulb,
hoed the corn,
rode the horse,
swam in muddy Missouri,
toed a dusty toad
with you
      green green green green
           you.

I'm in love with the way
the land loves you:
the way you greet
      morning wild rose
      afternoon fence post
      evening fire under forest leaves.

You show me how to walk
in the country dark:
      Black soil in waves
      under white moon Dakota.
      Black soil seep,
      sing Dakota.
      Black soil in your fingernails,
      white sweat on your forehead.

You speak of farmlights,
and the north forty.
You speak of choosing a home
by swimming toward it through river water at night
and judging whether you need to live there
by listening to the animal sounds on shore.

You move with light in you
toward me in the dark.
When you open your mouth and eyes,
light rides out of you toward me.

I no longer want to meet
people who have swallowed no living light from black soil.

Freya Manfred

Nebraska

WILD PIGS

There's four square miles of timber, mostly oak,
just north of here; the only stand of trees
much bigger than a wind-break up or down
the county, and it's thick as thatch, so thick
two fellows shot themselves by accident
just getting through the brush along the road.
The place is full of deer, and pheasants, and quail
like swarms of horseflies in a dairy barn.
And, listen up: they say there's pigs in there,
wild pigs, the size of hunting dogs, with tusks
that'll snap a fellow's shin-bone like a twig.
The story goes that in the Civil War
some farmer from Missouri drove them here

to keep the army from conscripting them.
They say he fed them acorns through the war,
and when he went to drive them home again
in '65 they wouldn't go. No Sir;
they liked those acorns! Oh, he tried and tried
to get them out; hired herders, set a fire,
shot some of them for something, God knows why.
Although he caught a few of them, some stayed
and multiplied, and got as wild as wolves.
They're up there now, if anybody'd look.

Ted Kooser

FUNERAL AT ANSLEY

I write of a cemetery, of the
perpetual care of buffalo grass,
of kingbirds, catbirds, and
cottonwoods;

of wild roses around headstones,
with their high thin stems and tight
tines, their blooms pursed in
the morning.

I write of old faces, of cotton
hose and flowered dresses and
mouths which grew up on
the weather.

And I write of one woman who
lies a last time in the long sun of
August, uncramped by the wind which
autumns each one of us

under catbirds, kingbirds, and
cottonwoods, and the gray-green
leaves of the buffalo
grass.

Don Welch

Kansas

MOONLIT NIGHT IN KANSAS

The plains of Kansas stretch out
under the moon like a sheet of music.

Buffalo lie bleeding in the grass.
The sound of their panting
rolls along the Kaw River
like the beat of ghostly tom-tom.

Arcturus descends
andante molto cantabile.

The sons of the homesteaders
have migrated to Asia.

Their daughters went east
to enter the Miss America Pageant
and were never heard from again.

An old Indian recites
meaningless words:
Topeka, Manhattan, Wichita.

Victor Contoski

Colorado

WATCHING JIM SHOULDERS

When did my manhood wake to its dying!
Never in New England or in Elko, Nevada, inside
screen doors with legal girls, dulled by fifty-cent splits.
But in Colorado's air and snow like first communion lace on
blunt mountains. He was Mantle on horseback, the
same class, and as injured, out of that remote private
America of ranges, ranches, vast wide-open space where
sophistication is silence. Truth is your action shot
from corrals, lasso wrist flicked instantly with
eight seconds to rope and tie or lose. Shoulders,
scraping the cheeks of steers along earth cut by
grooves of his boot heels, while those horns that could
cave in ribs, turned until the folds in the animal's
neck looked like its spine would split through skin,
yet didn't in this master's hands.

Leo Connellan

ANTHROPOLOGY IN FORT MORGAN, COLORADO

Tonight in Fort Morgan
girls are gunning
their convertibles, with hard tops,
up and down Main Street—
they look me over,
they pass, commenting to each other,
young boys honk
in their old clunkers   calling me names
laughing to each other
none of them are stopping.

Now a girl from Montana   with glasses
buzzes me twice
she speeds as she waves at the corner of Railroad;
I'm standing across from Vern's Bar, my old Ford loaded
down   I get in and begin tracing their route
turning on Main at Railroad
past State to Prospect, then down
Beaver to Kiowa
left on Bijou to Main,
then around the circle again—whooopeee! Square Dance!
We drive twice around
I'm restless for Chicago—
the loneliness here is small. O Fort Morgan of the picturesque name
this dance,   this life is not very charming.

Sam Hamod

Utah

DESERT GULLS

When these inland gulls
swept down on fields black with crickets
the Mormons
thought them doves sent from heaven
to save their crops.

The green wheat took root,
ripened and turned pale in the sun.

Now the hills of wheat are gone.
No one remembers
that winter of Puritan endurance
when hunger was not yet history
and the gift of white birds.

Once, plowing a field
on a forgotten island
in the Great Salt Lake,
a flight of gulls
swirled out of a cloud
and settled on the broken ground,
thousands feasting in the furrows
I had made. I stopped the tractor
and standing in that field
felt the miracle moving again

that brought a prophet
and his people
to their knees—
in a blizzard of doves.

Dan Gillespie

ABANDONED COPPER REFINERY

In rooms of stone
men thought these hills of slag
bright seed, black roots
gripping into a bedrock of profit.

Now the shell of the mill,
hollow as a worked out mine,
is silent
save for the chatter of birds
that nest in girders
under the sagging roof.
In a cold oven
two dogs growl and lock
in love.

Outside,
where the broken river

curves rich with the yellow sewage
of upstream cities,
on a mountain of black slag,
a lizard sleeps in the sun.

Dan Gillespie

Wyoming

THE HEART MOUNTAIN JAPANESE RELOCATION CAMP:
30 YEARS LATER

I

inverted exclamation point
a lone chimney
dotted by the sun

foundations of barracks
crumble with frost
and the assault of range grass

the fencing has collapsed

as a young prisoner
he paced this camp
cleared the far acres
now his farm

the shadow of heart mountain
eases across his boundary line
toward his wife's grave
ritual of the setting sun
renews his dedication to battle
with this arid land

II

his only son was killed serving
the u.s. army in viet nam
mistaken
the letter said
regrettably
for a viet cong

III

how do lovers meet
a nisei farmer
a widowed ranchwoman

smiling in cafes with others
"do you still love me?"
"i wouldn't be here if i didn't"
whispered then slipped in folds
between bowling scores and price of feed
"do you still love me?"

surrounded by the shadows
of heart mountain and its small towns
their silences burn like pine knots

campfire on a cold night

Charles Levendosky

OLD TRAIL TOWN, CODY, WYOMING

Where Liver Eatin' Johnson lies
in a second grave

and there's no admission charged
you can wander all day

through
the real remains
of those structures
once used
by fading frontiersmen

everywhere the grey-brown wood
deep-etched by mountain air
and piles of horse collars
and harnesses and all livery
stable paraphernalia
and spectral wagons
without horses
lined up in the actual ruts
of an old trail
which leads nowhere now

and the people from Pennsylvania
and Florida and Oregon and Ohio
walk solemnly through
in and out of the old saloon
the early settler's cabin
the old general store
under the awning where
the Sundance Kid
rested
and the dry Wyoming sun
drives down from North Fork
where the high Yellowstone Country
hides

On the way out
the sign says
donations
will be appreciated

John Garmon

THE GIFTS
For Minnie H.

when i offer the sack
of late apples
one of two
filled from your orchard
a gift of labor
to balance your gift of fruit

you say
"don't look around at my home
  don't look   i'm embarrassed"
meaning the earthen floor
and quilt over straw which serves as bed

you lean on an apple staff
to support accumulating years
woman as wizened as the windfalls
your sheep nuzzle out of the tall grass

i try not to look
that your grace not be compromised

the shaft of light
thru a chink in roof
falls at your feet

Charles Levendosky

Montana

A NIGHT AT THE NAPI IN BROWNING

These Indians explain away their hair
between despair and beer. Two pass out

unnoticed on the floor. One answers to a cop
for children left five hours in a car.
Whatever I came here for, engagement
with the real, tomorrow's trip to Babb,
the first words spoken 'white man'
split my tongue. I buy a round of beer
no phonier than my money is wrong.

Whatever story, I hear between the lines
the novel no one wants. A small aunt
whipped the brave who grovels now
in puke and odd hymns at my feet.
A squaw says no help from the mountains.
The Blood who stole her husband
breaks up all day in her beer. Children
drink us in through windows ten years thick.

It never ends, this brutal way we crack
our lives across our backs. With luck
we'll be soft derelicts. The next sun
is no softer, and I guess what good moons
must have said to them, some round white
ringing lie about the future—trout and kiss,
no ownership of sky and herds returning
fat from ritual songs. The moon outside
lights the alley to familiar hells.

And I, a Mercury outside, a credit card,
a job, a faded face—what should I do?
Go off shaggy to the mountains,
a spot remote enough to stay unloved
and die in flowers, stinking like a bear?

Richard Hugo

MY OWN BRAND

Frisco, Denver, Memphis;
no more brother Gene.
Portland, Albuquerque, Butte;
hell no the money don't show.
I ain't gonna roam.
Nights of broken bones.
Hotel homes; madness alone.
Can you spare a dime?
I ain't got the time!
Goddamn, rain in my boots.
The boxcar hoots. Jesus
these skidrow eyes, a bum's pride.

Valley home, a country wife;
that's what I'm a looking for:
smell of bacon in the morning,
a lady's downhome evening smile.
Kids calling me pa, a good wheat stand,
a few shade trees, a good stand.

That'll be my highway hope—
a few cattle down in the draw,
a missus to call ma. Yeah,
not so much really. A place:
a few chickens, a cow, a hog,
some garden corn, a good bull.
A soul full of cowpuncher pride.
Alfalfa, saddle horses, a hay barn,
pigeons flying all around.
A moonlight ride, a neighbor
coming by to shoot the breeze.
Or just fixing fence;
digging the post holes.
And a pond, rainbow trout on the line.

A little free time.
A couple drinks downtown.
Maybe once in a while be a clown.
Put on a show for the old fellas;
some rope tricks, bull-dogging,
a rodeo song. That's all I need:
a little prairie feed. A helping hand;
a chance to put on my own brand.

Art Cuelho

Idaho

CHRONICLE

It is January 12
and midwinter, the great dipper
stands on its handle in the sky
over pocatello.
The air, a presence
around the body when I go out
the door to relieve myself
is well below zero.

Yes it is well below.
This land is well
below, say shoot it, longitude
and latitude, yet it stings
like the Yukon, and standing,
to get back to that,
I thumb my nose several times
at the city below, it is midnight
and the lights are stationary
through the cool absent fog.

Inside Fred plays his cello
and that air sings thereby.
I run my fingers through my hair.
Here, all around, is
the world, out
on points, on the horizon are
friends close and far gone.
With the tautness of those
chorded strings bind them
together,
this air will kill us all
ere long.

Edward Dorn

Alaska

THE TRAIN STOPS AT HEALY FORK

We pressed our faces
against the freezing glass,
saw the red soil
mixed with snow,
and a strand of barbed wire.

A line of boxcars
stood open on a siding,
their doorways
briefly afire in the sunset.

We saw the scattered iron
and timber of the campsite,
the coal seam
in the river bluff,
the twilight green of the icefall.

But the coppery tribesmen
we looked for had vanished,
the children of wind and shadow,
gone off with their rags
and hunger
to the blue edge of night.

Our train began to move,
bearing north,
sounding its hoarse whistle
in the starry gloom of the canyon.

John Haines

THE INVADERS

It was the country I loved,
and they came over the hills
at daybreak.
                    Their armor
hoisted a dirty flag to the dawn,
the cold air
glittered with harsh commands.

Up and down the roads of Alaska,
the clanging bootsoles,
the steely clatter of wheels,

treading down forests, bruising
the snows—
                    bringing
the blossom of an angry sundown,

their cannon and blue flares
pumping fear into the night.

John Haines

Washington

DESERT HOLY MAN

Old Charley Garber delivered ice
to all the whorehouses in Spokane
when he was young
He had to admit the broads were good to him
but what a start in life
for a mystical philosopher
a yogi and a vegetarian

Charley did a Navy hitch
worked cargo in Seattle
helped build the San Francisco bridges
and moved machinery in L.A.
where he got mixed up with yoga
occult sciences and carrot juice

When his wife passed on
Charley came to Phantom City with his mind made up
to live the life of spiritual essence
which he mostly did
expect for playing poker with the firemen now and then
He was Chief and drove the fire engine
with a helmet on his long white flying hair
and his Viking whiskers blowing

Charley had a clunker truck
rigged up for desert prospecting
Weeks at a time he'd disappear
collecting rocks to cut and burnish
His shack was full of saws and buffing tools
blocks of rainbow agate jasper and onyx
pure turquoise chunks
blue crystal azurite and velvet malachite

Charley could work silver like a Navaho
belt buckles set with flashing stones
heavy necklaces and bracelets
rings with turquoise nuggets
but Charley was no salesman
He charged you what
he thought you could afford to pay
and loaned his money out
to every panhandler
He even set Kid Anaconda up in business
to be his competitor in town!

People thought old Charley was an easy mark
and took advantage of him
but Doc Odell went too far once
and said to some guys in the Silver Spur
as Charley walked in for a beer
"Here comes that old vegetarian son of a bitch"
Doc hit the floor so hard he bounced
Old Charley spit on his hands
and stood the drinks around

John Beecher

Oregon

DRAGGING THE MAIN

In the town by the sea I walked
Past the closed beauty shops where the
Hair-driers inside gleamed like bombs
And the manikins wearing their human
Hair didn't understand this game:
The cars drove round and round the

City blocks, their hoods and trunks
Leaded in and young eyes burned
Like radar above the red fires of cigarettes.

I looked through bakery shops and
Laundromats, searched the stark lights
The put-down baskets, the dizzy doors
For answers. I walked on as they revved
Away. We moved at our different speeds
Through rows of hot-dog stands,
Amusement arcades, pinball games, and doubled
Back. I saw the girl alone
In her car, and she turned to glance
At me. I thought the love that had
Once thrown me away was sneaking up
On four tires and about to say Honey

You get right in here. I waved.
She sped up and her taillight bobbed
Three blocks away through the mist.
I stopped under the marquee, turned
Again at the Watch Repair
Then saw her eyes again. They were not
Like those floating eyes of fish
That stared from the other cars.
She knew me, but something kept her
From slowing, and made her gawk and appraise.
She was brunette, and all by herself
And passed me five, ten, twenty times.
I waved from the bridge.

Each time I thought I'd lost her
Her gaze honked upon me once more.
Twice in the dark I raced her till
I stood where the Shell sign squeaked.
I breathed deep that perfume she left.
And was glad she helped to destroy me.

More and more she floated past in shadows.
I was chained to her recurring course.
I was faithful. She spoke to me
Lowering for once the window of cold
Glass and we were there by the roaring sea.
She said it wasn't love stinging my face
But only the pure cars of America that
Were dragging the main, looking for fools
Who want to hold even the lights of Main
Street, and the sweetness of a face.

David Ray

INDIAN PAINTING, PROBABLY PAIUTE, IN A CAVE NEAR MADRAS, OREGON

Over a trail glinting with flakes
of half-worked arrowheads, jasper, obsidian, flint,
I follow an Indian entirely to stone.
His cave clenches itself around me,
I am the eye of the cliff come back to its socket
to spy on this hillside of animals breeding and dying
and boulders losing their balance. In the cave of my mind
words form white like crystals,
What remains to be seen?
I twist to the light, but glare seals me in.

What remains? Indian, the dark at the back
of your cave stays where you left it, and cold rock walls
still bruise flesh upon bone: always we live
in between. I lie where you lay. Overhead
on the spalling sky, murky with soot,
arm's length away the elk you painted
runs on head down the color of my own blood.
You made the gory sun to shine above,

and over the sun strides a kind of man with a bow.
I lie and think of that hunt: man, elk, and sun,
tracing it over and over until your paint
seems to ooze down my fingers and wrist, and clot.
Indian, flat on your back in this cave you
made what I would, a prayer to your gods;
a sign to your people you were here
but left: I follow you into stone.

Jarold Ramsey

California

MARIN-AN

sun breaks over the eucalyptus
grove below the wet pasture,
water's about hot,
I sit in the open window
& roll a smoke.

distant dogs bark, a pair of
cawing crows; the twang
of a pygmy nuthatch high in a pine—
from behind the cypress windrow
the mare moves up, grazing.

a soft continuous roar
comes out of the far valley
of the six-lane highway—thousands
and thousands of cars
driving men to work.

Gary Snyder

HOW WAS YOUR TRIP TO L.A.?

Here in the North, our houses and their appointments
are old-fashioned and a little inconvenient. There's no doubt
that our lives here are morally
superior to those of the Southern people.

In the South there are many cars
The plumbing works, the gas stoves are better
Food's cheaper and the sun is warm
Unfortunately the air in that place is poisoned.

Our city tends to disappear in cold weather.

12:xii:63

Philip Whalen

CALIFORNIA #2

In the hour of Fresno
A strong blue
Yellow god
Valley of no rain
Afternoon walks
Full of wind from the
tips of the hills

Gypsy sings a song
And we walk toward
the car
And travel to the secret
two room dwelling
To laugh and sleep
on the floor

The Hispanic morning
of Aztlan
Welcomed with Café
con Canela.

Victor Hernandez Cruz

ANOTHER ACADEMY

how can they go on, you see them
sitting in old doorways
with dirty stained caps and thick clothes and
no place to go;
heads bent down, arms on
knees they wait.
or they stand in front of the Mission
700 of them
quiet as oxen
waiting to be let into the chapel
where they will sleep upright on the hard benches
leaning against each other
snoring and
dreaming;
men
without.

in New York City
where it gets colder
and they are hunted by their own
kind, these men often crawl under car radiators,
drink the anti-freeze,
get warm and grateful for some minutes, then
die.

but that is an older
culture and a wiser

one;
here they scratch and
wait,
while on Sunset Boulevard the
hippies and yippies
hitchhike in
$50
boots.

out in front of the Mission I heard one guy say to
another:
"John Wayne won it."
"Won what?" said the other guy
tossing the last of his rolled cigarette into the
street.

I thought that was
rather good.

Charles Bukowski

THE SONG OF THE MEAN MARY JEAN MACHINE

Strapped to the roof rack of her
silver mint Carrera: a surfboard
and a bobsled and boxes of live
pheasants and rabbits for her hawks.
It's the Mean Mary Jean Machine,
the green flag on pride, a one-lady
field guide to Western birds!
She wears a crocheted white wool
cottage industry Guatemalan power
hat, and a cottage industry purple
cotton Guatemalan power shirt,
and her custom yellow shades are
perched on the power hat like
a Gold Eagle's eyes. On the seat

beside her, two Russian Wolf Hounds,
and in the back, in custom leather
tote bags, a black M-4 Leica,
a one-eighty Blad, and a big mean
peregrine on its perch.
                          Whoooeee!
Here she comes, shooting the California
mountain passes on her way to her song!
This lady's lyric is in the point spreads,
somewhere between a redtail on a bunny
and a goshawk on a jack! She's up
to her bumpers in leaf mold, and
getting it on up to the brag!
                          At her
ten-dollar-a-head concert they sell
stickers that say DON'T SHOOT HAWKS
and THE MEAN MARY JEAN MACHINE—

                                          all

the money marked for Bangladesh.
She feeds more hungry people
than the church.
                  Call it whatever,
it's a kind of paean, the American
love song of the Mean Mary Jean Machine.

James Baker Hall

Nevada

RENO, 2 *a.m.*

Campers from Fayetteville & Toledo,
Winnebagos from Des Moines,
divorcees at the tables
with their souvenir spittoons.

And even when the stars are out
you can't see'm for neon and pollution.
Sequin G-strings and gold lamé,
feathers of birds no one dreams of eating.

A fat man drinks another freebee
and drops a flivver on Little Joe.
No one has much to say, no one
talks the weather.
None speak home. They dream of California
as tho from here
there is no where else to go.

Sam Hamill

THE MAN WHO INVENTED LAS VEGAS

In church he never felt the
weight of God which hangs
in those places heavier than

any mist; he only felt
the overwhelming presence of
luck. When he knelt, his bones

cracked like loaded dice and
fell into place. The choirs
he heard were of roulette wheels

spinning in rooms velvet
and vacant of light as an
altar without candles. He saw

middle-aged housewives
grown tired of marriages more
sour than lemons standing in rows,

pulling the levers of slot
machines again and again, often
not seeing the final combinations

of their unexotic fruit. The
fascinations of boredom and
chance! He gathered electricity

and with its flashes and spurts
and steady rays turned darkness
out of the desert forever,

thinking *we shall never sleep*.
He witnessed the spectacle
from a distance, and in

the trance of a child staring
into his first fire,
learning the beauty and heat of

its rage. And he thought not
that it was good or bad, but
that what he had made

was a thing some of the people
who live on earth for a while
could believe in.

Gerald Costanzo

Arizona

CROSSING THE COLORADO RIVER INTO YUMA

It is almost dusk.

For a long time,
we've been travelling.

I saw a hawk
flying low against the sky.
The horizon was stone.

That was only a while back.

No one owns this river. Wash with it. Drink it.
Water plants with it. Pray with it.

The evening sun glimmers across the desert.

Colors signal memories
of past journeys.

Sounds filled everything
and overflowed
upon returning.

Now, the river is silent.

The Greyhound bus roars smoothly on the bridge.
The river bed is hot sand. The willows are last weak vestiges.
Alongside the river bed is a concrete canal.
The liquid in it flows swiftly, directed, and lifeless.

A brown man leans
by the Yuma bus depot wall,
a daze in his eyes.

He tries and tries
to smell the river;

he leans,
trying to feel welcomed
to his home.

*Yuma is a small town. It abounds with modern Americana,
motels, gas stations, schools, churches, and etc. Where
did they all come from? Do they really plan for survival
this way?*

Neon is weak.

Concrete will soon return
to desert.

Be patient, child, be kind
and not bitter.

Prepare for the morning.
Go down to the river bed.
It will let you.

Sing a bit, be patient.
Wait.

Simon J. Ortiz

JULIO

He wanted
a pickup truck
to drive
across the reservation
never had the money
so old broken knife
retired from the indian police
traded his
for two bottles of port
it had no tires
no motor
and took four mules
to haul it
over to Julio's
front yard
where it sat
in the sand
next to the boulder
with the word
FUCK
painted on it

He used to go out in the morning
and touch it . . . get drunk
and sit in the driver's seat
herd his family out to sit
in it on Sundays
when he died
they moved it over
his grave
wrote on it
in english

"Here lay Julio
   He were crazy for Truck."

Kell Robertson

SPRING

Ice has been cracking all day
and small boys on the shore
pretending it is the booming of artillery
lay prone clutching imaginary carbines.

Inside the compound returning birds
peck at bread scraps from the mess hall.

Old cons shiver in cloth jackets
as they cross the naked quadrangle.
They know the inside perimeter is exactly
two thousand and eighty-four steps
and they can walk it five more times
before the steam whistle blows for count.

Above them a tower guard dips his rifle
then raises it again dreamily.
He imagines a speckled trout
coming up shining and raging with life.

Michael Hogan

AT GRAND CANYON'S EDGE

Eating the eggs for a buck eighty
In the Bright Angel Lodge
I think of the Indians
Who held out down in the canyon
While the Colorado sluggishly
Dumped again and again its tons
Of snow and bullets and arrowheads
Mud and fishscrapers, skulls
Fishscales, coins, and dark hair.

Out the picture window
Beyond the waitress in her yellow
Plaid I can see the red rocks
And juniper. The gnarled old tree
Blows out
Over the mile deep canyon.
Indians stood there, on the ledge
And thought and thought
About our kind, who'd come
In snow, with skin white
And hard as clay bells,
With voices that rarely chant.
They watched the Colorado flowing
Away. They watched the sunset
Move away. They watched
The white man approach, shaking
His rattles.

David Ray

New Mexico

HOW TO GET TO NEW MEXICO
(for Nicanor Parra)

First, turn left at the Old Oraibi Bar. Then, at Mexican Water
drop off Defiance Plateau. After Window Rock, if the
grocery stores change to igloos with rainbows for screendoors,
you'll know you're close.

From this point on, wear only mud & snow tires.
Shift cautiously from high to low. Don't count on overdrive.
Miles here will be measured by sidereal time.
Steer clear of leaded gas. Beware of dervishes & ghosts.

If the number of cows & donkeys on the road
bewilders you, jog a sharp right, hit a left, climb the Divide
stumble twice over your own heart, then examine your head.
When the mountains resemble sphinxes, if mice blow from
the top of your brow, don't pass Gallup
without a cup of coffee at the Uranium Cafe.

Now then. Because rains come suddenly, take care
of mud steeples falling against the fenders of your car.
Peel your eyes for lacquered saints running through tumbleweeds
along the shoulders of the main trail.
And don't let stray cemeteries steal your view.

It's dangerous to peer downward while in dialogue.
It's better to steady your breath with the altitude.
In Arizona be suspicious of echoes that holler back.
In New Mexico watch for gods disguised as
night janitors in flat-roofed bakeries. Notice that all
the inns have doors leading only out.

Are you wary upon your arrival?
Wish you might have ventured north instead of south?
Gone to Colorado? Taken a side-route through Mexico instead?
If you feel tilted even though standing straight,
or become lost in Albuquerque, go immediately to the corner
of Fourth & Shangri-la.

Inspect the magnets in your coatsleeves.
Are they pointing towards the clouds? Have the coyotes
stolen your favorite hat? And how about your feet?
Feel like they're anchored to several loose oceans?

When night falls, bundle warmly.
Destroy all previous concepts before going to bed.
Keep your thoughts in tune with your respiration. Tease
no one with the ends of your fingers. Wrap all dark sunnes

carefully. Now dig a slender cavity & defy
the forces of gravity.

Above all, beware of owls.
Don't leave your shoes off guard.
Keep in mind that heaven lies in some profound arroyo.
That what you mistook for soft clusters of dung & marl
are really the homes of men. That goats under the moonlight
turn green. That children riding hummingbirds may at
any time pass with flagpoles through your dreams.

This is New Mexico.
Tomorrow when you rise, clean your pockets bare.
Get ready to retract what you've always held in common.
There are wild dogs yelping under your bed.
And angels with bent wings ready to bite you.

Now look in the glove compartment.
Find a map?
I thought so. Do you still need it?
Bueno. You're all set.

I can leave you now.

John Brandi

SANTO DOMINGO CORN DANCE
                Santo Domingo Pueblo, New Mexico

Each beat of the drum's a round drop of rain,
the stamping of the dancers' feet is rain,
their heartbeats and breathing resound as rain,
the fringes on the men's moccasins are rain,
their feathers are iridescent sheets of rain,
the toes of the barefooted females are rain,

the women's hair runs thick with black streams of rain,
the billions of motes of dust underfoot are rain,
the chunks of turquoise a lighter shade of rain
than each needle in hundreds of evergreen sprigs,
the links and clasps and rings of silver are rain,
the ghostly Koshares' antic movements are rain,
even the billions of beams from the sun become rain,
and then the actual rain, onto the earth,
for the corn, O always the actual rain,
there it comes, then it comes, and it comes.

R. P. Dickey

LANDSCAPE, NEW MEXICO

A blue pickup
bounces along
dust rising behind it
up the wide canyon
into the dark.
Two Indians, drunk
reel to the top of a hill
watch until
the blue spot is gone,
laugh, punch each other in the mouth
celebrate the end of anything.

Kell Robertson

WHEN THE FAIRIES

When the fairies come back to Santa Fe
they sit in dark caverns called taverns
and eat nervously picking at their food.

When they come back to Santa Fe
they gesticulate nervously and it's London
is meant.

When you pass their tables you see
their fingers flying off from Santa Fe
to Dakar or somewhere very far
away where neither you nor they
have ever been.

Still, they are nervous and pick at their food.

When the fairies fly back to Santa Fe
coming in on their smelly little wings
they gesticulate and Paris is meant
and they play games like guess what
book is meant,

and what color

and order drinks no one can mix.

They are a witchy bunch
and very inarticulate and late
in the day they order a lunch no one can assemble,

which they attack nervously
guessing what color—
where Copenhagen is meant

guessing what color and raiment.

Edward Dorn

THE INDIAN GRAVEYARD

The carnival was a sick,
drab place. "Buy real Indian food
(made with canned beans and Bisquick)
and see the Indian dance

(in feathers from Woolworth's)" White
men with Lone Ranger eyes
exchange rifle shots for animals:
kuddly koalas and the lot.

Someone from the East laughed
at the Indians who were
stuffing themselves with hotdogs.
"The good Indians are over there."

And so they were. The graveyard
was filled with Indians
below ground. Plastic flowers littered
the mounds; no real greens

grew on them. Some real Indians
lay within, I guess, although
with names like Stanislaus Chiago
and Bernice Mary Garland

I wondered, and walked to where
the graves had no names:
furrows silverfished the domes
of the mounds; green fur

clung to the crosses. Stoicly
these Indians (their grandsons
drink Italian Swiss Colony,
Thunderbird, or Gallo;

get killed in wars or go
to work for the gas company)
spoke a gaunt rhetoric;
never said how.

Ramona Weeks

BETWEEN A GOOD HAT & GOOD BOOTS ·

"When you've got a good hat
& a good pair of boots
what lies between
will take care of itself."
Clarence said that
over his fifteenth beer
away from his wife
who won't let him drink at home.
His children gave him a hat for Christmas
brown, twenty five dollar stetson
hand creased
& his wife came into the bar
& told him to go home
almost exploding with the words
& he answered her quietly
said he was sorry
went out into the parking lot with her
slapped her once alongside the head
& came back in to
finish his beer.
He drank till closing time
played pool & told stories
about driving a herd of cattle
through the village of Placitas
in 1937.

When he came in a week later
he wore a battered straw
sat in a booth by himself
drank three quick beers
& left in a hurry.

Kell Robertson

Texas

CROSSING WEST TEXAS (1966)

Ranching country
            real ranches
not as in California
where a station wagon & an acre
is called a ranch
            but a whole day's riding
to cross one man's land,
flat & grassy
governed by levi-clad millionaires
policed by hard eyed youth
still playing cowboy
doing cowboy
            as in work
would tree a town
if possible
            work hard all day
& go home to read
Zane Grey, Luke Short
now & then bounced to town
for a movie, a western

In the thin towns
taverns are still saloons
longhorns over the door
on the jukebox, the Sons of the Pioneers sing
Cool Water
                    "Old Dan & I
                    with throats burned dry"
perpetuate
our own legend
                    sixgunned in pickups
across this hard country
where a man can shoot his wife legally
if he catches her fucking
                    O Lord our
Mr. Johnson came from Texas
                    a cowpunched president
reeking of barbecue
who taught school
                    climbed a fat dollar
stuffed the greasers & the poor white trash
into his wallet . . . started war on poverty
fired the first shot

West Texas takes years to cross
in an old car with the household
crammed in the back seat
sticking out of the windows
we are very careful
stop only for gas.

                                        Kell Robertson

DRIVING NORTH FROM KINGSVILLE, TEXAS

1.

Texas, you swagger in our veins.
There is no way we can get you out, or would want to.
I am addicted to these raw horizons,
vast sprouting plain where cattle gather in clumps,
this blunt edge on our lives.
Living here for so long we come to know our spaces.
Everywhere we look a new field soothes us onward.
Wild pigs skitter across the road.
Nothing scares us because we have so little to hide behind.
I am finding myself closer to whoever is driving this car,
whatever I do, whoever you are.

2.

In the last small town Raoul gave me his heart.
He wrote: "This is my heart. Put it in your pocket."
A strong square man offered up poems like gentle soufflés.
The Gonzalez girl, hard as a seed when she entered our class,
has softened and cried.
You are not easy to leave. None of you.
Texas will never be easy to leave.
It has whittled us, smoothed our splinters,
given us names and places and hollows like a wooden spoon.
We stir up dust across the long blank heart, caring.

3.

At Len's Pic-A-Rib outside Three Rivers
a cowboy gnaws barbecue like a hound.
I drive by at top speeds
and see him through the screen door,
hand to his mouth.
For a second, he is as real as I have ever been.
For a second, he is all of us,
hats on the table,
making ourselves at home.

Naomi Shihab

AT THE AIRPORT IN DALLAS

At the airport in Dallas, you come down
out of the air, and I think
that's the terminal with the escalator
that doesn't work.
There Dallas is, or rather
Texas, like an old Greyhound
Bus Station, all the guitars
on the seats, and boys in high heels
going back and forth to the john,
with a map of the world on the floor.

But it's a foreign country,
all the same, nobody as bored
as they ought to be,
walking, walking to the counters,
getting the local schedules,
everybody trying to get there,
or trying to leave.

And a lady in a pink chiffon dress
with a mink stole,
who keeps calling out
to a little blue velvet girl,
You just come right back here,
Lucille.

Stephen Mooney

JEFFERSON, TEXAS

The hotel register claims this used to be an exciting town
Now it's withering up like a grandma's hands /
used to knit, now can hardly do buttons

The drugstore waitress is young, her face a closed pod
She delivers my cup silently
it's noon / one customer measuring cream

As I loiter around the paperbacks
the girl washes my cup, instantly, she was waiting for it /
waiting to slick her counter with a damp rag

Is this how we die? One cup where there might be six,
her eyes watching me leave
as if I just stole all the sugars

Outside the wind blows
a crow sits in a window,
stands on one foot, then the other

No one passes
A sign in the chapel tells me to give my life to God
In Jefferson, Texas

you don't need to look both ways
before you cross/
you just cross

Naomi Shihab

Oklahoma

COUNTRY-WESTERN MUSIC

The further it comes,
the more dry grass
it has to crackle through,
the more it means.
Three in the morning—
Oklahoma, cricket down the road,
women listen
all along the line.

Ted Kooser

HE TOLD ME HIS NAME WAS SITTING BULL

he told me his name was sitting bull
the great-grandson of the old chief
and he reached across my arm
to fill his glass
from the pitcher
that is his excuse to sit closer

"where you from?"
          he is from southwest oklahoma
          i am from the northeast part
"i have been looking for you for six
hundred miles" he tells me
and the grassy plains near anadarko
he spreads out for me in the brown skies
of his eyes
          i smile   hiding my teeth

between the branches of oaks that
spread their leaves in tahlequah

"come with me" he squeezes my arm
the sioux horseman rides away across
                    my shoulder
i shake my head
and drown his horse in the water
of the illinois river

the young warrior drops his hand
but he never surrenders
his name will follow me on the interstate
all the way into the center of oklahoma

                    Joy Harjo

A CHOCTAW CHIEF HELPS PLAN A FESTIVAL IN MEMORY OF PUSHMATAHA'S BIRTHDAY

We know he liked chockbeer and watermelon
and raced sleek ponies in the dead of night.
We'll give him that. We'll have to open up
the valley to whites and those Chickasaws,
or it's sure no go. But we'll keep it pure.

Now for the other games, let's see, we'll want
the local P T A to have free rein to
search Muskogee archives for stickball rules
and rituals of the eagle dance and how
to mourn his bones, old style, for channel eight.

A lot depends on image. Use your masks.
Don't wear boots. Speak the language if you can,
or invent. And let's have them see us pray.

About the chock: keep it out of their sight.
And strip all the kids under nine or ten.

One more thing: we can get those federal funds.
So look dumb, play poor, form car pools or walk.

Jim Barnes

THE LAST SONG

how can you stand it
he said
the hot oklahoma summers
where you were born
this humid thick air
is choking me
and i want to go back
to new mexico

it is the only way
i know how to breathe
an ancient chant
that my mother knew
came out of a history
woven from wet tall grass
in her womb
and i know no other way
than to surround my voice
with the summer songs of crickets
in this moist south night air

oklahoma will be the last song
i'll ever sing

Joy Harjo

Missouri

In all the midwest
everything's moist.
The summer season
begins to announce
itself as lord, and
my tight Levis hang
on a nail more now.
I use a Missouri
roadmap for a fan
and wear my shoulder
into a sweat from
fanning my forehead.
The humidity is rank.

I've been to three
auctions this week,
bought an iron, a
frying pan, both hot
items, and some other
stuff, critical junk;
have helped unload
two big trucks—day work,
in old loose pants,
safety-pin strong;
circled a country pond
scaring frogs off the bank
with my woman, and saw
a bluebird, a bob-white,
and a young rabbit nearby,
and—was it a muskrat?

Almost hit a blue-racer;
breathed country road dust
that didn't settle onto
lacquered-looking leaves
or queen anne's lace or
wild roses through air vents
of our old green Pontiac.

And, knowing (as if it were
a juicy secret) I had
air conditioning at home,
if only in one room,
hung around too long
at all three auctions;
and criticized the coolness
of my woman's driving
a bit too much
because the car was hot.

R. P. Dickey

RIVERFRONT, ST. LOUIS

On the levee the Saarinen Arch
petitions luck for St. Louis
once and for all.
Cartons of trash
released from the Steamer Admiral
move in file on the Mississippi
with a kind of reverence.
Between cobblestones on the landing,
I discover a Roosevelt dime
blackened by many waters.

John Knoepfle

Arkansas

TOAD SUCK FERRY

One of the other things
About rivers
            is the crucial business of how you get across
Them.
Give them every chance
Give yourself every chance
To connect.

We, for example, take
                    ferries
Instead of bridges
And we drive miles out of the way to do so.
Once there was the sign: "Toad Suck Ferry, 30."
Laughing and pleased with the name we hurried
Off down the road some thirty odd miles
Out of the way across flatlands mounting low hills while
The sun flattened to a dull red at our backs.
Finally, we pulled up at a sign with the facts:
"Toad Suck Ferry: Closed at Sundown."

Well, it was down, the sun, and there was nothing around
And no one
And no sign of the
                    Toad Suck Ferry
Just the grinning gravel landing ramp, empty,

And the wide water,
The wide silent Arkansas.

Sadly, we retreated to the merest bridge
Possessed only of the delight of the name

Cheated of full right to claim it ours, yet
Metathesizing and jumbling joyfully for days,
We playfully fondled the phrase:
Toad Suck Ferry   Toad Suck Ferry

H. R. Stoneback

THE JUDGE

Let me tell you about your land:
four junk cars on it   blackberries
instead of motors   but parts a-plenty
for my lawnmower   and a rear-view mirror
for my truck   the best persimmons
grow here   and three big pear trees
that blossom white and fragrant
near an old shack I've stripped for boards
(I left one wall intact for the fieldmouse
and her babies)   best blackberry thicket
in these parts   sweet hay where J. D. Yarbrough
used to graze his cattle   a stream

Your land in November looks like
a Chinese print   all those stark trees
in the mist   blackjack oak and hickory
south of the stream   a pine grove
where I'd plan my mornings
I've seen deer   squirrels   quail
the remains of campfires   a small
junk heap of cans stoves refrigerators
that gave me a bookcase and shelves
for my potatoes   an old cart-road
where I ran my truck for the pleasure
of my son

and the place where Charlie Short grew marijuana
until the sheriff caught him   (you got him off
for the price of his land   a few weeks
before his suicide)   Clarence tells me
you came up here once in March   but thought
not to go with him to see your boundaries
huckleberries galore across the county road
where the mountain falls to the Mulberry
full of bream and cottonmouths   a spring
that even in August doesn't quit running
may-apples   walnuts   gin-seng   big trees
you sold for cabinets and tables

It's damned good land   Judge   you
got a bargain

Karl Kopp

ARKANSAS

I

Pine-tree boy breathing late-afternoon fireflies
       Beating out the rhythm of life
            on the back of a kitchen chair,
               the billet blues.

Caddo Mudfish served piping hot on a pie-tin
Annie Lou's joy juice, vintage year, Dalark's best.
       Beat out the rhythm of life
            on the back of a kitchen chair.

Fireflies trapped in boxes scattered down highway 7

       Yellow moon, Jassamine June
       Calling for the juba-elation

Steal Away, Steal Away—Uncle Buck's Back Room
   Calling for the juba-elation.

Pine-tree boy breathing last-flickering fireflies,
   Listening to the hymnals of glittered black-velvet night,
     While willows weep for the mourning dove
       and
     The Caddo croons a lullaby,
   Wend, wend a solitary path to home
       and
     Beat, beat, beat out the rhythm of life,
  Beat out the rhythm of life
     on the back of a kitchen chair.

         Jackman Young

THE NARRATIVE HOOPER AND L.D.O. SESTINA
WITH A LONG LAST LINE
    for Leon Stokesbury

One fall not far from Ozark, Arkansas
A gentle sheriff saw a hairy man
Upon the berm—hairy in the extreme
This man was, but kindly from his bearded face.
He hunkered there upon the fading grass
And to the sheriff seemed entirely at peace.

It's wonderful to see a boy at peace
So much he seems to love our Arkansas,
Even if he's vagrant on the grass,
The sheriff thought, who was a decent man,
Although not one to wear a bearded face,
Which faces were to him at least a bit extreme.

Could be this boy's entirely extreme,
A hooper flipped on dope and not at peace

At all with Arkansas—he'd have to face
This hairy one near Ozark, Arkansas,
To prove the Law is not the lesser man
Than one who is so fearless in the autumn grass.

And so the sheriff stopped his car, on the grass
And on the berm, in a state of mind extreme
For such a gentle and a decent man
Who lived in fact essentially at peace
With every normal man in Arkansas.
He parked, but showed some fear upon his razored face.

It was a moment all good men will face
In time, and man to man, on God's own grass—
We all must be in Ozark, Arkansas
Or somewhere just the same and as extreme
Some time, attempting to maintain the peace,
As honest sheriff or as gentle hairy man.

And so it was with our two friends. The man
Who had the hair on said, "Sheriff, your face
Suggests I've done some thing to break the peace
While taking of my ease upon the grass."
"I'm not exactly sure it's that extreme . . .
Are you a hooper?" the sheriff mumbled, then clearly saw

His man was nervous—"Boy, are you on grass
or L.D.O.!" His face was now extreme.
"Peace, Sheriff," said the hairy man, "I'm no hooper—I'm
from Dumas, Arkansas."

James Whitehead

GETTING EXPERIENCE

The first real job I got was delivering drugs
for Jarman's Pharmacy in Bascum, Arkansas.

If everyone was busy or in the back I sold things.
A cloudy woman with pentecostal hair

Softly asked for sanitary napkins.
She brought the kleenex back unwrapped in twenty minutes.

Shame said Mr. Jarman. We shouldn't make a joke
of that and made me say I'm sorry and fired me.

When I found out what it was the woman wanted
I had to say I did what they said I did.

That or let them know I hadn't heard of Kotex.
Better be thought bad than known for stupid.

The first hard fight I had was after school
with Taylor Wardlow West in Bascum, Arkansas.

Ward West chased me home from school when I was lucky.
My father said Ward West was insecure.

Go smile at him He said and let him know
you mean to be his friend. My father believed in love.

All day I smiled and twisted in my seat to see him
all hate and slump by himself in the back of the room.

After school he sat on my chest and hit me
and then his little brother sat on my chest and hit me

and then his little sister sat on my chest and hit me.
She made me so ashamed I tried to kick her

and kicked Ward West in the face. When he could see
I was halfway home. Jesus. Jesus.

Next day everybody told me over and over
how I had balls to make those stupid faces,

him the son of a bitch of the whole school
and how I surely kicked the piss out of him.

Ward had to go to the dentist. Also his father beat him.
He didn't come to school for two days.

Then he left me alone. He said I was crazy.
Everybody thought I was a little crazy

Although with balls. I just let them say I was.
Better be thought mad than known for stupid.

Sneeze, belch or fart. Choose if you have a choice.
Nobody's going to think you're good and sane and smart.

Miller Williams

Louisiana

PINE BARRENS: LETTER HOME

It could be Louisiana, attracting rain.
Soft ground, low land marshes creeping
into ragweed. These names own themselves.
Think of sassafras, a wildness never caught.

Black Lake with the cajun ladies, noisy nights
you woke me for fishing. The snapshot of dark

Campti shows a crying child, your wide hat.
Rowing the sucking water
you said, look for the dead men, watch now,
three went over the dam last week.

Mother, I think about the Blacks
who called at night, took you to their church,
baskets of beans we found on the porch.
I wouldn't touch your red snapper or stew.
But I've found crawfish in the pine barrens
of New Jersey, swamps bordered with ginger
root. And the people distrusting ties,
losing themselves the same.
Some recognition keeps after me;
I pulled away, now I can't forgive
my own survival. It's true I live apart
but like a root.

Your letters come asking for money,
catfish aren't biting, too much rain.
The garden swells with mud. The wide black walnut crashed
at Campti, lessons of moss collapsing on Black Lake.
Like other times you'll manage.
I've searched you for blame, for anger.
If I could, I'd drag back everything: husbands, sons,
years. But you say you love us all;
even departure is a sign,
the return is certain.

Cleopatra Mathis

VIEW OF LOUISIANA

The delta lies unchanged, flat
as childhood: a woman gathering pecans
from a yard black with water, purple martins
after mosquitoes, all winter mock lilac.

In the dream of wrought iron
you find them—the grandmother is fierce,
both arms waving you away. Your mother
takes your hand to speak
of fishing from low pine flats,
how she loves the nests of water.
She says your pride will be her death.
You wear your grandmother's wild name,
her fan of hair.

You wake to mountains: reflections
off coastal islands, hills of prairie marsh.
Memory is the first claim,
you'll spend your life coming back
to this flatness. By dusk you have forgotten
everything but the bleeding outline
of the river. You watch for New Orleans,
the white cluster of tombs.

Cleopatra Mathis

SOUTHERN SEASON

The straw bonnet
Thwarting flies and sun
Over the solemn old-maid face,
Its long ears down,
Is put away. The summer's gone.
The tinkling mule-bell
Has another sound that summoned
In the Spring the Persian look
Of jewel colors in the snowball jars
Or Roman candy and the trumpet call
Of Mardi Gras. The winter pall

Hangs in the air
Like a great fog on Chef Menteur
And slows the town
To the sad movement
Of mule-hoofs heard
On cobble stone.

The old man's head hangs down
Like the mule's ears
And grey dust powders his black skin.
The long, long street
Is captive of a spell.
It chills and calls
The lure of the impossible
Creatures moving without life.
Sparrows mark the wires.
The peddler's voice floats off
Faint and longdrawn-out
And freezing as the air
Yet whistle-clear:
"Stone coal . . . . . charcoal!"

The coal is piled so high
The tail-gate's up.
Cold eyes of houses stare
Then mirror black
And from some chant
In polar waste the echoes fall
To the measure of the cold,
Slow, clanking bell:
"COAL . . .
Charcoal . . . Stone coal . . .
S T O N E———————COAL!"

Alice Moser Claudel

MARDI GRAS

Me first
you all
the folks
tramping up
God knows
no one knows who
and our favorite dead
tramping up

everybody coming on
waving his balloon
overhead
black
orange red
anchored in his fist
floating by the least
long string

oh balls
of red white
and green blooming
up to say
it's springtime
oh say I'm
all right it's
springtime.

George Keithley

ALCIDE PAVAGEAU

Slow Drag Dead
halleluiah
four black Cadillac
high black hearse

and all
the people come
to hear the trom
bone bawl
look at Slow
Drag picture on
the Wall
He call again
Sweet Emma come
Big Jim come when He call
then honkie play
and honkie plunk
in Preservation
Hall

Miller Williams

Mississippi

PACHUTA, MISSISSIPPI / A MEMOIR

I too
once lived
in the country

Incandescent
fruits
in moonlight
whispered to me
from trees
of
1950
swishing
in the green nights

wavelengths away
from
tongue-red meat
of melon

wounded squash
yellow as old afternoons

chicken
in love
with calico

hiss & click of flit gun

juice music
you suck up
lean stalks of field cane

Cool as sundown
I lived there too

Al Young

TROUBADOR

Once a winter bayou child knew the green music
Of the heart twirled on the frosted vine,
Of the cabin's musical pot bubbling the greens
As winter cracked in a hiss of the old wood stove.
In the night's rock he felt the mother hugs
And the dark hymns in the lamp's yellow/black geometry.

Now dark belled as a melon mandolin
He came troubador to sweaty river towns,
Jazz hireling sunk in blue smoke and garlands of dance,
Fat musical druid priest jarring the Natchez docks,
A gay balloon dark-ragging among henna, banana, and tar
Casting blue streaks to moon

And often
He beat green wood Fourth-of-July speaker platforms black
With the stomping of his bunioned feet,
Sweated marbles under a red sky
As down in the hollow of his skull
He dredged forth the break-away tunes
Green from winter's bayous.

J. Edgar Simmons

DELTA FARMER IN A WET SUMMER

Last summer was hot and dry, a better time—
Two cuttings at the dock and two knocked up
In the fields, and a crop to fill the wagons full.
There were prime steaks and politics at night,
Gin to nine and bourbon after that—
By God, we raised some handsome bales and hell,
Then went to New Orleans as usual.

But now it rains too long, too little sun
To stop the rot. Rain beats down on the roof
At night and gives sad dreams—black bolls—
And the Thunderbird will have to go. You can smell
It on the evenings, like the smell of a filthy
Bed, or wasted borrowed money, the stink
Of a bloated dog when finally the water's down.

. . . in California they say it's dry.
They irrigate consistently, don't count
The weather in when going to the bank,
And that's damned smart, except they've got no woods
Or sloughs to crowd the fields, and dogs get killed
But rarely drown—and I think our bitch, stretched hide
And stench, contains the element of
      chance a Christian needs.

James Whitehead

Tennessee

THE BLACK BOTTOM BOOTLEGGER

Headlights bounce off
Light mist:
We drive Tennessee back roads
To Black Bottom
To the Black Bottom bootlegger,
Five refrigerators
Lining his neat porch.

He doesn't want last names
Though he tells the folks we're with
The weight he's lost
From haying
And of the cow who died
Of twins.

We find his prices good,
Seals unbroken
On brand bottles brought
From Nashville.
He doesn't trust us enough
For white lightning
(busthead)
But then,
We wouldn't trust to drink it.

From over the mountain
Half a moon
Stumbles into this hollow.
We leave
Loaded with heavy
Twisted paperbags,

Cold air rattling us,
And small stones
Under our feet.

Esther M. Leiper

TENANTRY
(Polk County, Tennessee)

Always in transit
we were always temporarily
in exile,
each new place seeming
after a while
and for a while   '
our home.

Because no matter
how far we traveled
on the edge of strangeness
in a small county,
the earth ran before us
down red clay roads
blurred with summer dust,
banked with winter mud.

It was the measurable,
pleasurable earth
that was home.
Nobody who loved it
could ever be really alien.
Its tough clay, deep loam,
hill rocks, small flowers
were always the signs
of a homecoming.

We wound down through them
to them,
and the house we came to,
whispering with dead hollyhocks
or once in spring
sill-high in daisies,
was unimportant.
Wherever it stood,
it stood in earth,
and the earth welcomed us,
open, gateless,
one place as another.

And each place seemed
after a while
and for a while
our home:
because the county
was only a mansion
kind of dwelling
in which there were many
rooms.
We only moved from one
room to another,
getting acquainted
with the whole house.

And always the earth
was the new floor under us,
the blue pinewoods the walls
rising around us,
the windows the openings
in the blue trees
through which we glimpsed,
always farther on,
sometimes beyond the river,
the real wall of the mountain,

in whose shadow
for a little while
we assumed ourselves safe,
secure and comfortable
as happy animals
in an unvisited lair:

which is why perhaps
no house we ever lived in
stood behind a fence,
no door we ever opened
had a key.

It was beautiful like that.
For a little while.

George Scarbrough

A FATHER IN TENNESSEE

dear son:

when you left us you left
gazebos, heat and buzzards,
a gravelled febrile Eden
for the city.

won't you, like poor Cowper,
write us receipt of your mother's picture out of Memphis?
did you ever see her knit under a moon?
do you recollect
the bled dread blood drops are hers?
can you remember barefoot
how here with us you once
struck a living hi and ho
come bang a letter from the savage blue.

I wade my poems, the salt in my eyes,
I glare around for the boy not there.
he is in the tiger ruins or rambling ancient skies.
how can I climb that slick steeple
lean from it, crying aloud new mountain sounds?
did you have a rotten journey of it?
And how was the war?
We are well there is no news.
Dad.

J. Edgar Simmons

AN EXAMPLE OF HOW A DAILY TEMPORARY
MADNESS CAN HELP A MAN GET THE JOB DONE

My brother knows the man
who really is Smokey the Bear.
I have seen a picture of him
wearing his other head
and smiling his human teeth
into the camera.

Days
he feels, walks, sweats,
and talks to campers.

Nights
he lives in Memphis
under the name of Simpson,
sleeping off the woods
and the smell of fire.

Mornings
he puts on the fur suit,
and goes to work
only a little madder
than the day before.

It is the stares he draws
driving
that keep him going.
The hairy head
slips over his,
and the darkness closes
around him, deep
and comfortable
as a growl.

John Stone

Alabama

PLAIN

Out of Mobile I saw a 60 Ford
fingers wrapped like pieces of rope
around the steering wheel
foxtail flapping the head of the hood
of the first thing ever
he has called his own.

Between two Bardahls
above the STP
the flag flies backwards
Go To Church This Sunday
Support Your Local Police
Post 83
They say the same thing
They say
I am not alone.

Miller Williams

LETTERS FROM BIRMINGHAM

Birmingham. The city bell tower chimes one.
I write letters from an all-night diner,
telling of the four hundred miles I've done
this day: rubble of roads and the weather,

the repairing of tires gone thin and flat.
The hawk-eyed waitress watches me writing.
She says I write with a fine hand except
for the extended slant. I cringe and bring

myself to straighten up beneath her eyes,
loading my letters with her small talk home.
What else is there to write of in the pose
of Birmingham, my hours in Birmingham,

the slick city hot on a Sunday night.
That my righteousness will overwhelm me?
That the intensity of my fire is great
and will sustain us all? Not that, I pray.

But from the bell tower I hear the singsong
pealing of "Dixie" windward by the hour,
the bell-rattled refrain of "Dixie" hung
blessingly over Birmingham, sky and spire,

tipping the Sabbath with hallelujahs
to worshippers spun from their homes at dawn,
hearing church organs grind out canticles
for all souls dynamited into heaven.

Harold Bond

Florida

CAUSEWAY
(Captiva, Florida)

Now that the causeway spans the channel
The venerable ferry is up for sale.
Mainland traffic edges out, bringing
Timetables, souvenirs, a new breed of trader.
The islanders go indoors, harboring their secrets,

But the birds line the causeway railing
To get a better view. Perched midway
Between tradition and progress, they enjoy
A little of both weathers, the dark
Ancestral green and the bright chromium.

Allan Block

CUBAN REFUGEES ON KEY BISCAYNE

Breathless when the breeze deserts them
    old men

              in aluminum chairs
              face the sea.

Their hands
    flutter in sleep

              their mouths fall open
              they are great, tired beaks.

They breathe,
they breathe!

              their sons have invested wisely.

Over the tangle of magenta and purple
    voice of birds
                in staccato.
                Mama is calling.

Imperious, final,
    she is a tambourine
                gathering her girls, black-eyed
                wrens whose ears are pierced
for tiny crucifixes.

Great hotels where old men gambled and kept whores
    are schools.
                Gulls circle Veradero
                with cries.

Barbara Winder

HEROES OF THE STRIP

Muckers drive muckers' cars
old Buicks, beat-up Pontiacs
with dented grins and eyes that pop
glaring from rusted sockets.

Muckers love their cars
purple crimson body jobs
sporting banners, raccoon tails
and on the dash or back seat
dolls that light up, bob.

They go really fast
the muckers and their cars
blast off like rockets
spew exhaust. Muffler shot
they weave yaw cut you off at the pass

then white walls grabbing the concrete
they skid to a stop
and from the rear window a skull nods, glows
just to let you know
a mucker and his car are ahead of you.

They have the air of having been
and got through many a tough spot
on the strip. Saturday nights hungry for more
the muckers and their cars rev up.
Watch out you hard-assed Cadillacs
Jags Porsches goddamned foreigners
you don't know what love is.
They shout and gunning motors roar
into the parking lot of the Dairy Queen.

Sheila Cudahy

Georgia

WRITING ON NAPKINS AT THE SUNSHINE CLUB
MACON, GEORGIA 1971

The Rock-O-La plays Country and Western,
 three for a quarter and nothing recorded since 1950.
A man with a heart tattoo
had a five dollar thing for Hank and Roy,
over and over the same songs
till someone at the bar asked to hear a woman's voice.

All night long I've been sitting in this booth
watching beehives and tight skirts,
gold earrings and bracelets

glowing and fading in the turning light
of a Pabst Blue Ribbon sign,
beer guts going purple and yellow and orange
around the Big Red Man pinball machine.

All night long a platinum blonde has brought beer to the table,
asked if I'm writing love letters
on the folded napkins,
and I've been unable to answer her
or find any true words to set down on the wrinkled paper.
What needs to be said is caught already
in Hank's lonesome wail,
the tattooed arm of the man who's all quarters,
the hollow ring and click of the tilted Red Man,
even the low belch of the brunette behind the flippers.

David Bottoms

FAITH HEALER COME TO RABUN COUNTY

Seldom is the tent full, but tonight he expects the local radio
to draw a crowd, also the posters up for weeks
in barber shop windows, beauty parlors, convenience groceries.
Even now his boys are setting out extra folding chairs,
adjusting the P.A. for more volume, less distortion,
wheeling the piano down the ramp of a U-Haul trailer.

In the back of a red Ford van he goes over his notes
on the healing power of faith:
the woman of Canaan whose daughter was rid of a devil,
the lunatic healed who fell no longer into fires,
the Sabbath healing of the withered hand,
the spitting into the eyes of the blind man of Bethsaida
who first saw men walk as trees
and then after the laying on of hands, men as men
walking on legs among the trees.

Even now he can smell the sweat, the sawdust, the reviving salts,
feel the healing hysteria run electrically through charged hands,
hear the quivering lips babble senselessly into the piano music.
Who would be healed, he will say, must file to God's altar
and stand in awe at the laying on of hands,
or those unable to be in the congregation
need only lay a hand on the radio,
withered as the hand may be it will be whole.

And if all goes as he prays it will go
even the most feeble will quake down the sawdust aisle,
kneel or fall unconscious at his shocking touch
to rise strong, young, healed in the spirit.
There is medicine in the passionate heart, he will say.
There is medicine in the power of God's love
O Jesus, Savior, touch this sick brother
who accepts in faith the things we cannot know
O sisters come to the altar, lay your hands on the radio.

David Bottoms

DOUBLE-HEADER

Each and every one of us
has got a schedule to keep.
—a truck driver being
interviewed on radio

I've made it
have been left alone in the stadium
locked here after the baseball
twilight game, having hidden
where I won't tell

on a bet with someone I invented
and therefore had to win.

I can hear the Security Guard
locking up, watch him making his way out,
turning off the lights as he goes

toward home and supper, away from
the smell of popcorn and beer.
I can see him look
with a question at my car,
the only one besides his

still in the lot and see him
look back once at the stadium without
knowing or even thinking I could be
looking back at him, my face barbed
with wire. I turn now to the stadium

that is all mine, bought
with my money, purchased with
a three dollar ticket for the top tier,
the stadium that is coming alive again
with the crowd that is coming back

but of course isn't coming back
to watch me play, with DiMaggio in center,
Cobb in left, Hornsby at second,
Rizzuto at short, and all the others
who have been tagged out more than once

themselves, and who will get me later
or sooner, trying to stretch a single
into a double, catching up with my lost breath
that I can remember now from when
I was eleven, with a stitch in my side

sprinting still in spite of the stitch
for the inside-the-park home run
I almost had when I was twelve

for the girl I almost got when I got
old enough but didn't know the rules

dusting my pants off now
to the music I never learned, for
the symphony orchestra I never conducted,
my hands rough with rosin
for the truck I never drove

and the fish I never caught
and wouldn't have known if I had
how to take him off the hook,
for my father who is in the crowd
cheering out his heart

but who of course isn't there
as I pull up lame at second
with a stand-up double
in this game that goes on for hours,
my hands stinging with the bat,

the All-Stars aligned against me
in this stadium I own for the night,
one great circle and inside this circle
this square that seems the only one
on this curving darkening ball of earth

or the only one anyway
marked by bases I must run all night
for everything I should
by now
be worth.

John Stone

South Carolina

There shouldn't be a North
Carolina, it is all
South. Stopping here
by a ditch, a corner
gas station abandoned
for years in high weeds
with a boxcar rusty and on
blocks behind it,
doors chained for cargo
they've forgotten, one notes
only by chance
before getting back into
the car the huge and
rusting chains hanging
from the cottonwood,
gross, giant, sneering
tree. Its shade
is a remnant of that darkness
in which they gathered
from their fine fields,
their breath afire like dragons.
Their laughter vanished down
the four roads, tobacco
men blind and blending into
history. And no one can prove
anything—there are so many
crimes to rush on to.
It's only a hunch,
as if a man still swings
heavy and burning from that tree.

David Ray

THE EVANGELIST

Each summer, the alien evangelist comes
to do for us
what we cannot do for ourselves.
Sometimes, he is from Memphis;
sometimes, from Tucson;
but always his skill is superior.

Bennie Lee Sinclair

DECORATION DAY

This first Sunday in June, this green
first Sabbath of June, has long been designated
for the cleaning of graves. Each program
is the same: everyone brings rake, hoe, some
flowers, and, after preaching, climbs

this stubbled hill to find wiregrass
and weeds have taken ground since June's
first Sunday past; wild vines
and briars choke the rose and dahlia
left of last year's tending.

Each pilgrim as of age assumes his role:
the old knead deeply in ancestral
dust, upending spiny threats upon
their own sure home, while those of lesser
urgency resolve themselves unmossing faded

elegiacs. It is the young who take
no part. Escaping one by one to ride
the afternoon, they do not hear the gentle chime
of hand-tool hitting rock; this knelling
for green bones as well as brittle.

Bennie Lee Sinclair

North Carolina

MY GRANDFATHER'S FUNERAL

I knew the dignity of the words:
"As for man, his days are as grass,
As a flower of the field so he flourisheth;
For the wind passeth, and he is gone"—
But I was not prepared for the beauty
Of the old people coming from the church,
Nor for the suddenness with which our slow
Procession came again in sight of the awakening
Land, as passing white houses, Negroes
In clothes the colors of the earth they plowed,
We turned, to see bushes and rusting roofs
Flicker past one way, the stretch of fields
Plowed gray or green with rye flow constant
On the other, away to unchanging pines
Hovering over parallel boles like
Dreams of clouds.

            At the cemetery the people
Surprised me again, walking across
The wave of winter-bleached grass and stones
Toward his grave; grotesques, yet perfect
In their pattern: Wainwright's round head,
His bad shoulder hunched and turning
That hand inward, Luby Paschal's scrubbed
Square face, lips ready to whistle to
A puppy, his wife's delicate ankles
Angling a foot out, Norwood Whitley
Unconsciously rubbing his blue jaw,
Locking his knees as if wearing boots;

The women's dark blue and brocaded black,
Brown stockings on decent legs supporting

Their infirm frames carefully over
The wintry grass that called them down,
Nell Overman moving against the horizon
With round hat and drawn-back shoulders—
Daring to come and show themselves
Above the land, to face the dying
Of William Henry Applewhite,
Whose name was on the central store
He owned no more, who was venerated,
Generous, a tyrant to his family
With his ally, the God of Moses and lightning
(With threat of thunderclouds rising in summer
White and ominous over level fields);
Who kept bright jars of mineral water
On his screened, appled backporch, who prayed
With white hair wispy in the moving air,
Who kept the old way in changing times,
Who killed himself plowing in his garden.
I seemed to see him there, above
The bleached grass in the new spring light,
Bowed to his handplow, bent-kneed, impassive,
Toiling in the sacrament of seasons.

James Applewhite

REUBEN'S CABIN

Looked stitched together and
patched with warping pepsi signs,
stilted to the ridge.
The rathides hung out to cure
under the eaves could have been
part of his random repair.
In the warm months he'd
sit by the river for days, pole
stuck in the mud, hunched back

under a tarp thrown over
a makeshift frame for wet weather.
That's why collectors rarely
found him when they climbed up to
his roughly scaffolded roost.
The story had it the girl he
married in the low country
went bad, and none of the children
long since gone were
conceived in his bed.
During the first World War Reuben
hid in the family's attic, then
after the armistice snuck out
and arrived at the depot
in uniform. Look, I've heard
Reuben rolled his cornbread
in little pills to eat and seen
him cuss my grandpa once when
he got up to testify. His wife
gone to hell, his piles,
the dirty pension.
Reuben what were you thinking
those long hours in the mud by
the catfish waters while
the schoolbus passed and returned?
The tarpaper on your roof has flown
down into the trees along the creek.
Your traps' jaws are
locked by rust where they hang
along the ridgepole and squirrels
have stolen all the innards from
your smelly couch. What
are you thinking now in the
silence circling up near Buzzard Rock?

Robert Morgan

HILL HUNGER

Lem Catlett had one pretty gal
along with all the ugly ducklings.
Sissy joined the WAACs, then magically
she became an air stewardess
and married a Texas oil man,
the way such stories should turn out.
The couple visited Bull's Branch once
in a pink limousine upholstered all
inside in unborn calfskin,
on the radiator a great span
of Texas longhorns running before.
They had to walk the last quarter mile,
the Ridge Road being too narrow
for their magnificent chariot to pass.
They took old Lem and Matt back
with them to Texas for a rest
(Lem had already rested sixty years).
Lem and Matt stayed one week, then rode
an express Greyhound back, hill hungry.
"That country's flatter than a damn
flitter," old Lem lamented.
"A feller couldn't take a leak
in his own backyard without
he was seen way over yander
in Oklahomie."

John Foster West

A PLACE BY THE RIVER

You take what it gives you, what a spinster
gave this farmhouse. Barren pear trees
remain of the land but the house
maintains itself with the life sunk into it,

seeming pious and generous
as the body of a sleeping saint.

Canning jars, calendars, a box of clothing,
letters, tracts and Bibles: in each object
her presence gathers
as you distinguish the woman in her surroundings.
She was brief, God-fearing,
suspicious of dying, cautious, certain
and sane. She kept Christ's picture
like a husband's or lover's
and a picture of Job articulating his pain.

In a room you lean by a window,
listening to a mockingbird in a pear tree.
You want to cup in your hands the voice like water
and drink or pour. A clear stream,
it winds mid-air from the limb through every room,
and you wonder if this was the tone of her strength;
if the keeper she kept within her whispered
in a voice so solitary.

You watch the bird, and in the distance between you
envision a winding, muddy river,
baptism by immersion and the glorious hysteria.

William Keens

Kentucky

IN THE CORN LAND

In the corn land I move up one stalk,
watching tears streak tree thighs in prison weather.
Wandering lost,
I spoke to a canopied beech on Knob Hill,

waiting an eternity for a reply from the
depository holding old echoes.

I move up another stalk,
then spider-like
rest to spin a web.
I cheer at the escape:
A lone catbird dive-bombing a slap-happy cicada.

Far down the snake trail
lively Saturday music of banjo and violin
shake Aunt Sally's pump-knot hair
into flowing cornsilk.

As the C & O freight, 20 miles away,
clack, clack coal dust into prisms of sun,
hickories drop scaly bark in early summer.

Thoughts fog my view over this trespassed land, as
the dead cornfield offers woodchucks
a welcome feast on bones of its husks.

Suddenly, the green-face boy
    (is it Milford?)
comes to me with the dusk
holding a yellow fish.

I turn away to watch the twins,
Cack and Mack, far below,
surrounded by birthing fodder shocks,
step off 15 paces from the diseased barn,
then shoot the Clabber Girl between the legs
with BB guns.

Why does Aunt Mattie keep ticing, ticing,
that them two bucks will grow up wild as
sassafras patches?

Quentin R. Howard

THE OLD ATHENS OF THE WEST IS NOW A BLUE GRASS TOUR

Lexington, dear heart, you old whore,
you didn't know you were for sale
until you'd been bought—rowdy
low-rent coal money named J. W.
in town on weekends for the game,
big Lincoln, tossing big bills &
quarters at your best fast dance band,
then passing out on the table—
the best Maître D' in town, he say
you can come back, but *don't* bring
your friend!
        But best Maître D',
he not our friend, he own the place
now, you know what I mean? I mean
he's our friend, sure (we nothing
without our friends, we all Nixon men,
even the women, and we don't talk about
life no more), but we save downtown,
some of it anyway, you remember,
fix up Vine Street, Gratz Park,
look at the 200 block of South Mill,
we saved a shitload of that old elegance—

James Baker Hall

STRIP MINING PIT

See where black water
slips down the broken spine
of rock,
down the ribs
of the hill, this stricken,

bony thing,
brown skeletal sprawl
stripped (efficiently),
by dragline
and digging rivulets of rain.
Rip it open
and the dark heart
gleams with promise,
with profit.
As thus, the prophet
sayeth,
lift your eyes
(to this wretchedness),
reach into
the rib cage,
grab a handful of heart
and run like hell.

Dan Gillespie

THE MAD FARMER STANDS UP IN KENTUCKY
FOR WHAT HE THINKS IS RIGHT

There he is crawling stomach and elbows across the frozen field,
apples in his pockets, binoculars tucked in his coveralls.
The mad farmer is a writer, teacher, naturalist, and family man.
He rests in his trek and eats an apple, shakes his fist
at the weekend warriors practicing bombs on the countryside.
The mad farmer drives a Scout, wears galoshes and a cap
with ears that tie under his chin. He gets a headache
when he goes to town twice a week to teach. Cincinnati money
has bought the next farm for hundred foot river front lots.
The mad farmer is under attack also by friends and family,
for being a communist, a reactionary, a liberal, a revolutionary,
a patriot, a cop-out, and a dangerous influence on the youth.

He makes it finally to the knoll, and sure enough, there they are,
wood ducks on the slough: there are dozens of wood ducks on the
    slough!

James Baker Hall

TOURISM

They come in search of front porch
washing machines, feuds, moonshine stills,
Long Mile, Stinking Branch, Slaughter District, Putrid Hollow,
Daisy Abner, Span Gussey and his kith and kin—the gaunt,
unfriendly natives and potbellied children who slide like shadows
between razor-back hills, barn dance frolics, ecstatic preachers
    battling
unadulterated sin;

they find what they're looking for, and much
more. We lay it on. In season and scheduled right,
they can hit such to-dos in some town every weekend:
folk festivals, promotors find, are an ore
to be exploited, and a little fun at the foreigner's expense
perfectly legitimate. To recapture our past
for a couple-a days takes a year's coordinating.
Preserving quaintness, we also take credit for
proper weather, full-house motels, increased coffers
on toll roads.
        Satisfied they found Appalachia, tourists go
carrying off the woman's club,
glossy printed at churns and quilts and wearing garb
freshly antiqued. They miss lone-standing chimneys crowned with
    birds—
landmarks of long-gone cabins and of love affairs between ourselves
and the earth—and go, believing they find us in the well-staged
    parks.

Lillie D. Chaffin

THE RETURN

All she took from her land
was a rose sprout, the meadow patch quilts
and a pack peddler's guitar,
given to her that day in blue,
with raspberry stain on her hands.

Her wish to return grew into the
hardest diamond of her years,
cached in the safest alcove of her mind.

"A home is built with rafters of memories,
stones of love and windows of desire."
A peddler told me that once, she said.

Left alone in a place that is not one's childhood country,
a journey is the easiest thing to take,
and one morning beyond the great clumps of
asparagus and lavender hedge the land looked
young to her.

Haddon, a son long dead, drove a flock of geese
up from the creek and she spread her white apron
to their screams.

Bruce Bennett Brown

West Virginia

78 MINERS IN MANNINGTON, WEST VIRGINIA

Thanksgiving. They have
taken a sample

of the air,
have found ample

evidence of Carbon Monoxide.
Somewhere
in that air
there are
78 miners. If they are alive,
it is a miracle,
& no one will save
them now. It is a simple

matter of sealing off the mine
to stop the fires
& the explosions. The wives
knew it all along,
it comes with the territory,
but found it impossible

to admit to themselves.
News comes frequently
from the Mannington, West Va.
mine, but there are no rumors.
Over the clotheslines,
white ropes dividing
the air with parallel lines,
women with stringy hair
refuse each other's mornings.
Their wooden clothespins are
held tight in their lips;
dungarees shake out
their knees & pivot slightly;
early morning dew
keeps the sheets damp.
But there are no rumors.

Day after Thanksgiving. A new
explosion rocks the mine.

Some say this is not a poem,
but what does that have to do
with the 78 dead miners
of Mannington, West Virginia?

Louis Phillips

Virginia

i went to the valley
but i didn't go to stay

i stand on my father's ground
not breaking.
it holds me up
like a hand my father pushes.
Virginia.
i am in Virginia,
the magic word
rocked in my father's box
like heaven,
the magic line in my hand. but
where is the Afrika in this?

except, the grass is green,
is greener he would say.
and the sky opens a better blue
and in the historical museum
where the slaves
are still hidden away like knives
i find a paper with a name i know.
his name.
their name.

Sayles.
the name he loved.

i stand on my father's ground
not breaking.
there is an Afrikan in this
and whose ever name it has been,
the blood is mine.

my soul got happy
and i stayed all day.

Lucille Clifton

HARD TIMES, BUT CARRYING ON

His eyes were once blue and pure
as the Bay, but that too
turned thick with grim
trails of tasteless oil and shapeless

carps of paper whose words, bleached,
seeped away on the slow flow.
He owns the same boat, boots,
and seine he started with forty winters

back, when running in and out alone was
possible blind drunk, on the nose.
He steers by a plain stick
and ropes; fancy wheels confuse him;

spits on the gilded engines that stutter
in bad weather, lacking control
even when all else is flush.
They ridicule the radar in his head,

the barometer in his bones, and shake
the air with sleek wakes. Even so,

he works his hole with craft,
eats fish for lunch at noon and dots

it with a single swallow of rye, then
drags back hard on the surging
net, while all around the bags
crank up slack as widow's dugs in rain.

Dave Smith

Delaware

AIRWAVES

The night was as sweet
as it was *there*.

Light rubber and hay smell.

"Thirteen-eighty Delaware Valley, W—A—M—S!"

A voice outside
part of the moonlight strips
on asphalt, in the fields.

You are outside ahead
and hands, feet, and car
follow red reflectors,
streetlights.

Three cyclists, like a school of delicate fish,
sway in your lights, darting home.

Warren Woessner

Maryland

NIGHT SONG FROM BACKBONE MOUNTAIN

Because you threw rocks at me on Backbone Mountain,
called me skinhead and my dog a bowlegged weasel,
don't come looking for me here to make up.
Go dig your own groundnuts if you can find them
    and onion weeds, and I hope
you choke on the buckbeans.

I'm nobody's fool, Jim Lewis.
I saw you lay her on the ground,
    your hands tangled up in her hair.
I saw you and I tried to run away
        up to Devil's Rock, up there
I watched her lead you back to town.

That is her way. I'm nobody's fool.
I know every bird here every leaf by names
    I gave them out of love, not
some name I stole from a book.
Every night I see the sun down
(you told me not to stare into the sun

    but still I go right on),
and I know my way by the stars.
No deer runs from me or wild turkey.
I live, I have been happy.
I'm nobody's fool but suppose I was
    and you were dead right all along?

A slant-toothed fool has his glory
    when banjos pick up in the bar,

and he dances for what dimes men toss on the floor.
They're his when he's done and gone home.
So long Jim Lewis.
I have been happy, so long.

Daniel Mark Epstein

FIRST PRECINCT FOURTH WARD

Every bar on The Block shut down.
Villa Nova, the Crystal, the Ritz and Midway,
dead neon, night flowers gone day blind,
eyes like a gutted steeple,
streetwalker with her make-up peeled clean.

The paradise is no more artificial
than the money paid out for it.

Get your morning hot-dog at Pollock Johnnie's
but don't ask for a drink.
This is the blade of justice untempered.
No truth in wine?
No more truth anywhere in town:
when a man can't get booze on The Block
at a reasonable hour, or an unreasonable hour,
when a sailor can't go for broke on East Baltimore Street
after a dry month at sea,
when a man can't get shot on East Baltimore Street
for minding soneone else's business,
a sailor can't get stoned, layed, blown and rolled
for his pay
then we must look elsewhere for The Republic.

Blaze Star, where has she gone,
and Lola, that up-side-down girl
and a hundred others that dance the drinks off the bar-tops,

and topless shoe-shine girls,
and the shades of countless women trapped in the photo
    peep shows?
They have all gone to the polls.

Jimmie the Greek is laying one hundred to one
    the President can't lose,
and the action is slower than a drugged clock,
    and may be slower.
But some people will bet on anything.

                        Daniel Mark Epstein

Washington, D.C.

SPRING IN WASHINGTON

The tourists arrive, swarming
over monuments, snapping Japanese
cameras on the Mall. Spring
leaps from the Potomac with the shad,
spawning in tidal pools and back runs.
Swamp crocus split, crack
open the dry sack of winter.

On the Hill Congressmen bloom,
April flowers in their lapels,
randy among the pert girls.
Paint gleams on the White House,
vacuousness grins among Senators.
A conference of dogwood convenes,
scenting the heavy air at State.

Mimosa and cherry blossom force
open the heart of the capital

of the free world, find frivolousness
green in the breasts of clerks.
All flags, initials, signatures
lose force, as the republic accepts
the *coup d'état* of spring.

James Den Boer

IT PLEASES

Far above the dome
Of the capitol—
                 It's true!
A large bird soars
Against white cloud,
Wings arced,
Sailing easy in this
humid Southern sun-blurred
                breeze—
             the dark-suited policeman
             watches tourist cars—

And the center,
The center of power is nothing!
Nothing here.
Old white stone domes,
Strangely quiet people,

Earth-sky-bird patterns
            idly interlacing

The world does what it pleases.

Washington D.C. XI:73

Gary Snyder

Index to Poets

For more information about the
poets, consult the following:

A Directory of American Poets
Contemporary Authors
Contemporary Literary Criticism
Contemporary Poets of the
   English Language
International Who's Who in
   Poetry
The Writer's Directory

Index to Titles

Index to First Lines